A DAILY CREATIVITY JOURNAL

365

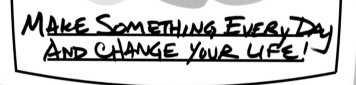

MAKE SOMETHING EVERY DAY AND CHANGE YOUR LIFE!

NOAH SCALIN

IF FOUND, PLEASE RETURN THIS BOOK TO

Cameron

_____

Voyageur
Press

DEDICATION

To my parents, Mim and Chuck, who encouraged my creativity even when it manifested as spaceship control panels drawn in permanent black marker under the stairs.

Quarto is the authority on a wide range of topics.

Quarto educates, entertains and enriches the lives of our readers—enthusiasts and lovers of hands-on living.

www.quartoknows.com

First published in 2010 by Voyageur Press, an imprint of Quarto Publishing Group USA Inc., 400 First Avenue North, Suite 400, Minneapolis, MN 55401 USA. This expanded version published 2016. Telephone: (612) 344-8100 Fax: (612) 344-8692

quartoknows.com
Visit our blogs at quartoknows.com

Voyageur Press titles are also available at discounts in bulk quantity for industrial or sales-promotional use. For details contact the Special Sales Manager at Quarto Publishing Group USA Inc., 400 First Avenue North, Suite 400, Minneapolis, MN 55401 USA.

10 9 8 7 6 5 4 3 2 1

ISBN: 978-0-7603-5008-9

Library of Congress Cataloging-in-Publication Data
Names: Scalin, Noah.
Title: 365 : a daily creativity journal : make something every day and change your life / Noah Scalin.
Description: Minneapolis, MN, USA : Quarto Publishing Group USA Inc., 2016.
Identifiers: LCCN 2015040520 | ISBN 9780760350089 (flexi)
Subjects: LCSH: Handicraft. | Creative ability.
Classification: LCC TT157 .S28 2016 | DDC 745.5--dc23
LC record available at http://lccn.loc.gov/2015040520

Acquiring Editors: Margret Aldrich and Thom O'Hearn
Project Manager: Sherry Anisi
Design: Noah Scalin
Layout: Cindy Samargia Laun and Rebecca Pagel

Printed in China

INTRODUCTION

A daily creative project is like a marathon. It's a ridiculously daunting task, but making an original creation every day gives you an incredible sense of accomplishment. It also forces you to push beyond your mental and physical barriers (especially the ones you've erected for yourself). You'll be amazed at what you produce and what you learn about yourself in the process.

363. Skullusion
My friends Nathan and Shelia endured several hours in a small dressing room for this shot.

When I started on my own year of daily art, making a skull a day, ending up on the *Martha Stewart Show* was the farthest thing from my mind. Indeed, I was really just looking for a new creative outlet. My year of art was a roller coaster ride that ended with a lot of unexpected outcomes, including winning the Webby People's Voice Award for Best Personal Website, writing a book, and giving lectures across the country. It also left me with a toolbox full of new skills and creative ideas, which I've already used in my professional design work and which I'm sure will come in handy for years to come. Even better, it helped me connect with my existing friends on new levels, as I worked with and learned from them, and even helped me make new friends from around the world. Most importantly, the project has inspired people to be creative, whether by starting their own daily project or just making one new piece of art.

OK, so "results may vary," but the reality is that the small, incremental steps I took every day added up to something much bigger than the individual parts. A daily creative project is something anyone can do with a bit of perseverance, regardless of skills or talent. And the suggestions and images in this book are designed to help you push past the things that can snag you along the way and to inspire you to discover what you are capable of.

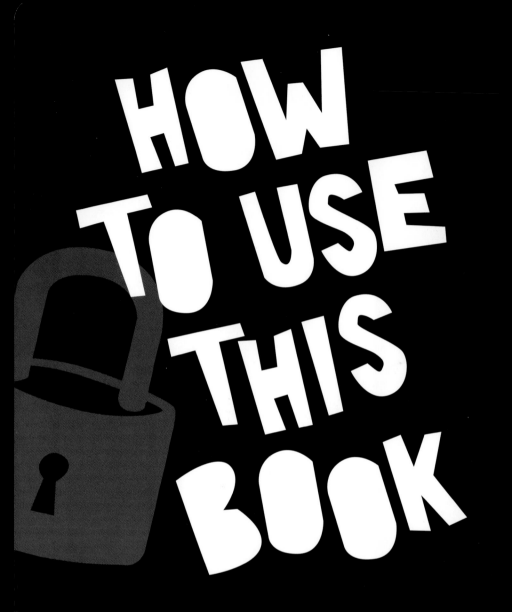

HOW TO USE THIS BOOK

The only rule is: There are no rules!
The point of this book is to put as many tools and as much inspiration into your hands as possible so that you have no excuse but to get started on your own daily project. Read it front to back, or just skip to the parts that interest you. Don't feel obliged to follow everything to the letter. If you feel inspired to do something completely different, go for it! A daily project is all about the rules you make for yourself, and there is no punishment for breaking those rules.

The journal part of this book is yours to do with as you please. I've written 365 project suggestions, but they are just that: suggestions. Feel free to ignore, rearrange, edit, and/or repeat as you see fit. Perhaps you'll even design an entire year's project around just one of them. While some are simpler than others, all of them are meant to be doable by anyone, with any level of previous creative experience.

Since my own daily project was visual, I've made suggestions from a visual standpoint. However, most of the suggested ideas can be interpreted for written or audio projects, and in some cases they are specifically designed for them. The blank spaces are for you to jot ideas, sketch plans, note experiences, scrapbook images, document your project, or just doodle in—it's all up to you.

Most importantly: Don't stress out. Remember, this is about taking little steps. When doing your daily project, focus on the current day and don't think about tomorrow, next week, or next month. Big projects can be incredibly daunting, but you'll be amazed at what you can do when you break them down into a series of tiny, manageable pieces.

And don't forget to share what you're doing! I want to help you do that, so please send an e-mail about what you're doing to me@noahscalin.com, and I will post about your project on the 365 blog: **www.MakeSomething365.com.**

Now get started already!

ABOUT DAILY PROJECTS

A yearlong daily project can be overwhelming— that's a good and a bad thing. The sheer scale of the task can make it seem impossible to accomplish, but it's that daunting quality that actually creates so many opportunities for incredible and unexpected results. Pushing yourself beyond your assumed limits is what it's all about.

For some people, just starting at all will be a giant hurdle. Others will dive right in only to discover that they're in over their heads halfway through. The problem (and also the exciting part) is that you don't know what you're getting into when you start a long-term project.

The concept of a daily practice isn't new. However, with the rise of easy-to-use Internet technology and inexpensive digital cameras, the concept has exploded. Suddenly anyone can easily share a project, gain an audience, and in turn inspire others to try it out as well. So what's the big deal? Doing something every day can change your life for the better, whether it's gaining a new level of skill, nurturing latent abilities, or just seeing what dedication and commitment can produce. And no matter what the outcome, you will learn more about yourself and feel a sense of accomplishment that's rare to find in our normal daily lives.

A daily project is a personal journey that can offer you a rare opportunity for self-discovery and personal growth with tangible results. And who knows? Maybe even a new career, a book deal, an exhibition, an extra source of income, or even fame and fortune.

CHOOSING A SUBJECT OR MEDIUM

The key to a successful daily project is deciding on a subject or medium that you will enjoy exploring for a year. Your ideas may come as a flash of inspiration, or it may be something you experiment with and research before settling on. Keep in mind that a simpler idea will go a lot farther than a complicated one, which can bog you down as it becomes increasingly difficult to produce.

If you choose a consistent subject matter (skulls, stars, smiley faces, Chihuahuas, etc.), pick something you already like. You probably have plenty examples of it in your environment to inspire you, and you'll be less likely to get tired of it before a year is over.

If you pick a consistent medium or technique (oil painting, photography, collage, etc.), this is your chance to take your skill to another level. They say practice makes perfect, and you'll be getting a lot of practice in the course of your project. Choose something you really want to master.

I enjoyed picking my subject and diving into the project but feel free to test out a few ideas before you commit yourself to an idea. Once you get going, don't be afraid to allow your subject or medium to morph. Perhaps you start with oil painting, but allow yourself to try other types of painting, or maybe you start with Chihuahuas, but move to other breeds of dogs as well. Let your interests guide you.

Once you settle on your subject or medium, you may find that you'll want lots of inspiration to help keep you going (especially after you work through all of the obvious solutions), so I've provided a short list of places to start on the following page . . .

SOURCES OF INSPIRATION

Check out these other people who created their own yearlong/daily projects when you're in need of some inspiration. You can find hundreds more on my MakeSomething365.com site as well!

Mask-A-Day   Gary Lockwood, AKA Freehand Profit, spent a year creating mask-themed art every day, inspired by my Skull-A-Day project. When he finished it, he spun off a successful career as an artist making masks out of sneakers, a technique he developed during his year! *www.freehandprofit.com*

Daily Drop Cap   Typographer and illustrator Jessica Hische made a beautifully crafted letterform every day for a year. The project helped her reach a new audience, and her typography is now regularly seen on book covers, in advertising, and even in movies. *jessicahische.is/awesome*

My Motivation   Design student Ashlee Boyd decided to keep herself motivated by completing an art piece every day based on words of creative wisdom she's encountered. The project created a passion for learning even when she's not in school, and she's already seen her work inspire her friends and bring her work opportunities as well. *mymotivationblog.weebly.com*

365 Days of Creative Canning   Megan Radaich spent a year canning and preserving fruits and vegetables in a variety of ways. Along with the therapeutic benefit of spending time by herself in the kitchen every day she also developed an extensive body of knowledge that she is now sharing with others through a new website, classes, and a cookbook of her own! *www.foodpreserving.org*

100 Hoopties   Daily projects don't have to only be for 365 days. Sometimes it's easier to commit to a shorter goal, and the results can still be transformative. Graphic designer and avid bicyclist Jennifer Beatty created one hundred days of reproductions of iconic posters using bike parts! The project went viral, gaining her an incredible amount of attention, but more importantly, she learned to get over a fear of failure and gained a better understanding of her limits and resourcefulness. *100hoopties.com*

365 Jars   Kirsty Hall spent over a year filling jars with unusual things and leaving them for others to discover. As a full-time artist, the project allowed her to learn more about her practice and figure out what she wanted to do in the future. She also pushed her own creative boundaries and learned about the power of letting go. Most importantly, she made deep connections with the fans of the project whose lives were impacted by their discovery of her work. *www.365jars.com*

SHARING YOUR WORK

It may be tempting to keep your daily project a secret, but having an audience can be an incredibly helpful and rewarding part of the experience. Why should you open your project up to public scrutiny? It may feel easier and safer to do it on your own, like a personal journal. Then there's no fear of judgment if you give up or something doesn't work out as you'd hoped.

So what do you gain from having an audience?

ENCOURAGEMENT A daily project is a hard task, and it really helps to have people encouraging you along the way (think of the people who cheer on marathon runners).

INSPIRATION People who followed my project gave me lots of good suggestions for things I could make and materials I could work with (sometimes they even mailed me those items, from as far away as Australia!).

ACCOUNTABILITY It's much harder to give up on a project when you feel like people actually care that you're doing it. I knew my readers were excited to see what I would come up with next, and in turn, that kept me excited to keep making new things for them to see.

SURPRISES A daily project can turn into a daily grind if there's no element of surprise, and an audience can bring things to it that you never imagined. Not only did my audience help shape the direction of my project, making it something much bigger than I ever imagined, they've kept it going long after I finished my year. Who knows what an audience will be able to do for you?

So what's the best way to get your daily project out there?

374. Snow (Day) Skull (with DudeCraft)
Even though my year of skull-making has ended, I continue to make skulls when the opportunity arises. This skull was created with my friend Paul; I even documented it as it melted away.

Technology is ever-changing, but the Internet is one of the easiest, most inexpensive ways to reach a potentially very large audience. You could choose to go analog and use the bulletin board at a community center or send things to a select group through the mail, but for practical purposes, a web-based project is going to be the best option for most people.

There are plenty of online tools you can use (see "Online Sharing Tools" for a list of resources); the key is not letting technology derail your project. If you're comfortable with a certain service, don't add learning new software to your to-do list. If blogging and social media are completely new to you, I recommend one of the free blogging options available, such as Blogger or WordPress. Both are easy to set up and use—just follow the directions on their sites. I created Skull-A-Day in 2007 in Blogger in less than five minutes and have never paid a cent to run the site since.

The nice thing about blogs is that you can always tinker with them later (Skull-A-Day went through three redesigns in its first year alone), so don't stress about what it looks like at the beginning. Make something simple so that you have a place to point people the moment your project begins. Just as you will acquire new tools and skills to complete your daily projects, you'll acquire new web tools and skills, too—as you need them.

ONLINE SHARING TOOLS

Technology is always changing, but there are several online tools that have been around for a while and are good bets for meeting your specific needs.

Blogger   A free blogging tool that allows users to quickly and easily create blog-based websites. The site also provides a large amount of free storage for images as well as tools for helping to share your blog through its large community. *www.blogger.com*

Facebook   A very popular social networking site. While not specifically designed for sharing projects, the site has plenty of tools that can be used to that end. *www.facebook.com*

Flickr   Allows for free storage, organization, and sharing of a number of images and/or videos. *www.flickr.com*

Instagram   For many people, the sharing part of a daily project can be harder than the making part. This app allows you to overcome some of those hurdles by quickly sharing images and video using your phone or tablet without needing to go to a computer.

Pinterest   An easy way to share your project documentation by adding images to virtual pinboards. You can then grow an audience for your project by interacting with the built-in community of users. *www.pinterest.com*

Tumblr   A super simple, free blogging tool with a built-in social network that makes it easy to start sharing your work without the complexity of a traditional blog. You can develop a community by finding and following other users and liking their posts. *www.tumblr.com*

Twitter   A social networking tool that only allows for messages of 140 characters or fewer to be shared with a network that you build yourself. *www.twitter.com*
> **Note:** *Adding a # symbol before text allows you to instantly connect with other people posting similar content. If you'd like to find other people doing daily projects, try searching the #Make365 and #MakeSomething365 hashtags.*

YouTube   A free video-sharing tool. If you have a project that features moving images or audio, this is one of the most popular sites to use. *www.youtube.com*

WordPress   Another popular free blogging tool. Allows quick and easy professional-looking blog creation. If you're looking to do long-term blogging, it's worth investigating both WordPress and Blogger to see which is best for you. *www.wordpress.com*

DOCUMENTING YOUR WORK

Daily projects can be ephemeral or concrete, but having a decent record of the results is a must, both for yourself and your audience. If you're working visually, one of the best ways to do that is with photographs. For many projects, this will simply mean photographing the completed piece, but if your daily project involves actions or creating temporary work, then documentation becomes even more important.

If you're doing a text- or audio-based project, you may think that you don't need photography at all. However, the Internet is still a primarily visual medium, and it helps to have images to grab viewers' eyes and keep them engaged with your posts. Why not take photos of your process or scan any notes you've made as part of creating your piece? Your audience will appreciate the glimpse into what it takes to get your work done.

You don't have to be a professional photographer to get a good shot. Most often, you'll want a straightforward image, and most basic digital cameras have auto settings that make a decent-looking picture. Keep in mind that shooting outdoors in daylight will make brighter, sharper images. If you need to shoot indoors, try using a flash or working near a window. Interior lights are generally dim and may need to be supplemented if you don't want to use a flash and don't want a long exposure (and a potentially blurry shot). You may find it worthwhile to invest in an inexpensive tripod to shoot small objects or things that are not well lit.

So why bother taking a good photo?

First, it's more appealing for an audience to look at well-shot images. Keep in mind that they weren't with you to experience the process, so this is their only way of seeing the results.

Second, you may end up using these pictures in other ways. Not only did I use my images in a book, but I've made T-shirts, prints, and other items. With the range of digital printing services available today, you can make some of these items on your own.

A few other things to consider when photographing your work:

- Shoot more pictures than you need. You can always edit down to the right shot, and you may discover that you need a different angle or version later.

- Review your pictures before moving on. You'll be much happier if you discover right away that you didn't quite get the photo you need and have a chance to reshoot.

- Take pictures of your process. It can be fun to share how things got done; taking pictures can even help you remember the details later.

- Consider keeping work that may change over time, and photograph it as it changes; sometimes things look better later.

- And don't forget to periodically have someone take your own picture in the midst of your project. You never know when it'll come in handy!

While photos are generally the most useful tool for documenting your work, you can try other things as well. A video camera can let you show your process or a project in motion. Audio recordings can document your thoughts as you work or even be the point of your project (how about a song a day?). Flatbed scanners can be used to document two- and three-dimensional work, and you can even create temporary work directly on the bed then save it as a scan. Have fun and experiment!

CAN'T FINISH YOUR PROJECT? YOU'RE IN GOOD COMPANY!

Can I tell you a secret? I didn't end up making something every day the first time I tried doing a daily project. I attempted to make a haiku a day for a year back in 2001. This was before blogging and social networking for me, so I ended up just sharing the work monthly on a website with a small group of friends. While I didn't stop partway through the year, I definitely had some lean months by the end. Regardless, I ended up with a huge amount of writing that I used for several years afterward: I created song lyrics for bands I was in and made a set of haiku postcards to promote my design firm that still turn up in stores and books periodically.

The funny thing is, I was well into the Skull-A-Day project before I remembered I hadn't been able to finish the haiku project. I credit opening up the Skull-A-Day project to a wider audience, and the support and encouragement that brought, with the fact that I never missed a day of skull making.

MOVING THE FINISH LINE

Not everyone finishes a yearlong daily project. Don't feel guilty if you want to give up—and don't be afraid to change the rules! So what do you do if you've started your project and find that it is getting too big for you to handle? First, you should congratulate yourself on getting started at all. Next, you have to make a choice about moving the finish line, whether by changing the rules, adjusting the time frame, or doing a combination of both.

If you find that the rules you set up at the start of your project are getting in the way or stressing you out, change them. Really, it's that simple. It's your project, and you set the parameters. Maybe you do something every other day instead of every day, scale back the size of what you're making, or even switch to a new subject matter or medium. See what elements are making it hard for you and adjust them to a comfortable fit.

If it's not a matter of the details, but a problem with the time commitment, then why not scale back to a shorter time frame? Perhaps six months, or one month, or even one week will make it more feasible for you. You may end up doing a series of shorter projects that add up to a year. Some people choose to make 365 pieces total, but at a pace that is more comfortable for them, with any number of days between pieces.

Regardless of how you adjust, you'll still be learning and growing along the way. Even if you just decide to stop altogether, don't discount the work you've done so far. You may be surprised when you look back and see how much you've already gained.

One final note on the subject: If you haven't begun your daily project yet, don't let the prospect of not finishing stop you from starting at all. Too often, people think and talk about all the things they could be doing but never take action. Just trying something new can do wonders for your perspective on the world and on yourself.

KICK START YOUR CREATIVITY

The following are some of the techniques and working methods that I found helpful during the course of my own yearlong daily creative project. I hope they'll give you a leg up on your project, even if it doesn't consist of making something visual.

FOUND OBJECTS

The thing about a long-term project is that the longer it goes on, the more you need to look for external inspiration. While I started out doing many of my pieces completely from scratch, as my project progressed, I often worked with preexisting items. I went to thrift stores, craft stores, and grocery stores specifically looking for items to work with, or I literally would find items on the street. You can start with everyday items, from candy to condoms and pretty much anything else you can imagine.

For an amazing bit of inspiration, check out the work of Terry Border at Bent Objects (www.terryborder.com). He creates incredibly clever and funny vignettes just using a bit of wire and everyday household objects.

330. Bent Objects Skull
Fellow blogger Terry Border made these figures then sent them to me to add a skull (out of ketchup, of course) and to photograph.

ADDING, SUBTRACTING, AND ARRANGING

There are three primary ways of dealing with preexisting materials. In broad terms, they could be considered **ADDING, SUBTRACTING,** and **ARRANGING.**

ADDING is basically another way of saying "decorating" in its simplest sense. Using common art materials, you can easily add something to existing objects. Paint, markers, pencils, and more can be used directly on a surface. Glues and other adhesives can be used to add other items to an object.

In most cases, you'll want to clean the surface you're working on before trying to add something new. If it's a particularly difficult surface to affix things to, try sanding it first. You may also want to cover the finished piece in a fixative, varnish, or other coating if it seems like your decoration might easily come off.

SUBTRACTING could also be called "carving," though that implies a more technical skill set than you need. Once you find the object you want to subtract from, mark the areas you want to cut out by drawing directly on it. Some materials will respond best to tools designed to work on them; try testing out your cutting tool on a small area before you seriously set to work.

Soft items like fruits and vegetables can easily be carved with household knives, though special pumpkin-carving tools also work well. If you want to carve harder materials, try using household tools that you already have on hand, such as scissors, drills, hammers, saws, chisels, and screwdrivers. If you want to get into extreme carving, consider investing in or borrowing a Dremel-type tool. These come with lots of special bits that can cut through just about anything, so use caution.

322. (File Under) Folder Skull

I stare at a bunch of these files on my desk every day, so I guess it was inevitable that I'd work them into my project eventually. It took a couple of tries to figure out how to make the simple cuts that would use the light and shadow most strikingly.

If you are going to cut up nontraditional materials, be careful that they and/or their contents aren't toxic. Goggles and a respirator are good safety tools to have on hand for this reason.

ARRANGING doesn't require additional materials, but it does take a bit of preplanning and a good eye for detail. Basically, arranging involves taking a number of items and putting them together so they look like something else. You can work large or small—the scale depends on the items you are working with. The more of an item you have, the easier it is to make something with greater detail.

The first thing you will need to decide is whether you are making a permanent or temporary piece. If you're making something temporary, choose a location that won't be easily disturbed, then spread out the items you're working with on a large, clean surface. Push the items around until they start to take the form you want; you can fine-tune the shape by removing or adding items as needed. When your piece is finished, be sure to document it, since once you clean up, that will be the only record of its existence.

If you want to make something permanent, make sure you start with a sturdy work surface, as that will become part of the piece. Since the items will be affixed, you won't be able to adjust as much as you go, so you may want to begin by drawing, lightly in pencil, the outline of what you're trying to create. Then it's just a matter of affixing the items with whatever substance makes the most sense, such as hot glue or wood glue. Once you're done, erase any of the outline that is still visible.

In terms of creating the image itself, there are two major ways to deal with large quantities of objects: organized or disorganized. There's no judgment implied, they each have their own appeal. Basically, you can pile things haphazardly on one another for a more jumbled look, or you can lay things side by side on one flat plane. As with all of this, there are no steadfast rules—just try things out and don't be afraid to start over.

COLLECTIONS

Working with collections of objects is an extension of the "arranging" technique. The items themselves can create a certain amount of interest with their unique or unusual details, so you might want to play up or reference those special attributes in your finished piece.

Since collections often have value, using the nonpermanent method generally makes the most sense. You can use your own collection or someone else's, if they give the OK. I got to arrange a bunch of old watches, play with knickknacks at a thrift store, play with the stock of a comic book store, and handle dozens of butterfly specimens. It goes without saying that you should work extra cautiously when the items are not your own, but be sure to explain beforehand how you plan use the collection so there are no nasty surprises along the way.

302. (Who Watches The) Watch Skull(?) My friend Mimi, who owns a store filled with all kinds of wonderful vintage clothing and objects, let me use her space and merchandise for many projects. In this case, she let me borrow a bin filled with old wristwatches.

COLLABORATION

My project started out as a personal creative activity, but it didn't take long to realize that such a large task isn't something easily done alone, nor should it be. If anything, the project became a great excuse to spend quality time with friends and make new friends along the way. You can ask for help with an idea you already have, or you can pick someone to work with and see what comes out of having a conversation about your project. You never know where things can lead, and that's what's great about it.

Recently I connected with a fellow blogger, Paul Overton at DudeCraft (www.dudecraft.com), and after a few e-mails, it was decided that he would come to my hometown and we would do a project together. We'd never met in person before but ended up having a fantastic, creative weekend together.

223. Recycled Ring Skull
I decided to turn an old ring into a new one, and my friend Tere helped make it happen. She taught me how to cut, bend, and weld the metal to make this skull ring.

LEARNING NEW SKILLS

As mentioned before, one of the things you discover in a long-term daily project is how quickly you use up all of the skills you already have. This may seem like a bad thing, but it's actually a great opportunity for creativity.

By learning new skills, you'll fill your personal creative toolbox with new techniques and methods that you can use once the

317. Sewn Skull
I drew the basic outline in pencil directly on the fabric then used a sewing machine as a drawing tool. Holding my finger over the reverse button and using a series of short taps on the foot pedal, I made zigzagging lines. Note that this method is a bit rough on the sewing machine!

project is over. In my case, I did one of three things when I needed a skill I didn't already have: I asked a friend to teach or help me, I took a class, or I simply read about it and gave it a whirl.

There's no reason not to just give something a try. To be clear, I almost never got something right the first time. Very often I would make things over and over until they came out they way I wanted: Finger painting? Over a dozen attempts. Japanese brush painting? Forty-five attempts. Drawing with a laser pointer? Sixty attempts! It may sound a bit daunting, but the end result was always worth the effort, and I had fun in the process.

NEW ENVIRONMENT

While working on a project every day, you can't always control what environment you're in. It's one thing to create something at home where you have access to your usual tools and materials, but being in a new environment can be challenging. Once again, this should be considered a positive rather than a negative. A new environment offers opportunities to find fresh inspiration if you're open to it.

When you're away from home, on a vacation, business trip, or day trip, consider bringing some easy-to-work-with materials, like chalk, scissors, tape, and/or construction paper, in case you get inspired. I frequently went to New York City during the course of my year and often had only an hour between meetings to create something. I did everything from drawing on the sidewalk to decorating construction barriers to cutting up flyers and newspapers. And you know what? I never once got stopped or harassed—people just assumed I should be doing what I was doing and usually paid no attention!

You don't need to wait for a scheduled trip to take you out of your usual environment; you can make trips specifically for your project. Need an excuse to go to a park, visit a museum, or take a bike ride in the country? Now you've got one.

WORKING SMALL

There are a lot of good reasons to work small when doing a yearlong project, not the least of which is the fact that if you're making physical objects, you'll need to find a place to put them all. By the end of my own year, every surface in my house was covered with the skulls I'd made. It looked great, but sometimes it was a bit overwhelming to visitors who didn't know what I was up to!

There are challenges in working small, since it may be difficult to hold, mold, cut, and/or glue materials that are tiny. When I worked extremely small, I kept a magnifying glass on hand and had a bunch of improvised tools to help me out. There's no need to buy special contraptions—tape or binder clips can hold things in place, pins can be used to mold things, and the smaller blades of a hobby knife will allow you to do a great deal.

Part of the fun of making small things is showing how small they are, so consider documenting them next to larger versions of the same thing or familiar objects (your hand, a coin, a ruler) that will give a sense of scale.

WORKING BIG

Making really large things every day may not be realistic, but once in a while it's worth the extra effort. The end results can be remarkable and make a big impact.

339. Video Fan Skull
My friend Erin, who works at a local video store, kindly allowed me to come in before working hours to make this piece.

First, consider if you want to make something that you will keep or not. If it's going to be a permanent creation, consider where it will be made, where and how it will be documented, and where it will be stored. If it's a temporary piece, you will have to work out how to recycle or return the pieces when you're done.

A fun way to do really large projects is to get other people involved. Use it as an excuse to have a party with an activity besides sitting around and talking. On one day of my project, some friends and I had a picnic in a park and then made a skull out of large rocks that were clogging a drain there—so we even did something positive for the community as part of the process.

TRADITIONAL CRAFTS

I learned a lot of new skills during the course of my project, and many of them were traditional crafts that I had never tried before. There are plenty of resources for learning crafts online and at the library, but you can also ask friends or relatives to share their knowledge.

Craft stores usually sell kits and instructions for common crafts, though I highly recommend using them for inspiration only and making your own individual creation. For instance, I took a latch-hook kit and designed my own image using the same color palette.

One word of warning from my own experience with crafting: The crafts that seem the easiest can also be the most time consuming. Plan to make something simple if you want to get it done in one day.

258. Cross-Stitch Skull
For this project, I created a grid on cross-stitch fabric, marked where I wanted my stitches to go, and then began making the stitches. I had never done cross-stitch before, so I didn't realize how time intensive it can be. This ended up taking eight hours to make, so keep it simple if you want to try this out in a day.

TOYS

Good toys are made for creative play, but most people put them away after they've reached a certain age or have them around only for kids to play with. A daily project is all about creative expression, so playing with toys again makes a lot of sense. Toys like Legos, Lincoln Logs, Tinker Toys, Etch A Sketch, and the like are perfect for making unique creations and are infinitely reusable.

This is a great opportunity to get children involved in your project. Young people are filled with creativity and can get you energized. Just remember that playing with toys is supposed to be fun!

PLAYING WITH FOOD

Possibly the favorite and most frequently used material in my yearlong project was food. There's something really satisfying about working with and transforming the things we eat, and food offers an almost unlimited range of colors, textures, and shapes to work with. You can use just about any technique described above and can even add nonedible materials. Best of all, you probably have all the tools you need already in the kitchen or at the table. And if you're careful when handling your food, you can still eat it when you're done.

352. Skull Roll
My friends Ross and Oura, who work at a local sushi takeout restaurant, kindly offered to let me invade the kitchen and create my own custom roll. They taught me the basics of sushi making, and I worked only with the regular ingredients they had on hand.

On the whole, food-based items are going to be temporary creations. However, the transient nature of food can add another dimension to your pieces. Why not document them as they age and transform over time?

MAIL ART

While e-mail has all but replaced old-fashioned paper mail, there is a thriving community that specializes in creating art that is mailed. "Mail art" simply takes a few stamps and an understanding of basic postal regulations. You can make art that conforms to the size and shape of a standard letter or work on preexisting postcards and envelopes, or you can experiment with the limits of what's possible to mail. Most harmless items can be mailed, even without packaging. Smooth pieces of wood can be used as postcards; soccer balls and coconut shells just need addresses securely taped on the outside; as long there's nothing hazardous to postal workers, there's a good chance it'll make it to its destination.

You can send things to friends or strangers, remain anonymous or let people know it's from you. A lot of folks do reciprocal mailings, where they exchange items with each other. There are even websites listing addresses of people who want to receive mail (Postcrossing is one well-used service: www.postcrossing.com). The fun part about mail art is that you automatically share your work with someone else—just be sure to document the piece before you send it.

ABOVE AND BEYOND

As you can see, a daily project is a wonderful excuse to push yourself to try new things, interact with friends new and old, learn more about your environment, and just have fun. The time you spend on a daily project will reward you in countless and often unexpected ways.

Regardless of the outcome, you will discover you've been changed by the experience. I constantly find myself using the skills I developed during my project now that it is over, and the friends I made during the process have added another dimension to my life. I also have a record of a year that I remember in more detail than probably any other year I will ever live. Most important, I finished my project with an added appreciation for the opportunities for creativity and happiness that are contained within every single day. I hope you'll find all of this and more in taking on your own project.

OK, IT'S TIME TO GET STARTED!

Here, you'll find 365 ideas to kickstart your creativity every day. Scribble, sketch, or jot down your ideas here; tape or glue stuff in it; or even make your project between the pages—this book is meant to be used!

The first step is the hardest, so start small today and make something that fits in the palm of your hand using only the materials in your immediate environment.

DAY 1

What's your favorite animal? Use it as your inspiration today.

DAY 2

DAY 3

Make something out of paper, but *don't* use scissors or glue or draw on it. What now? (And no, you don't have to know origami to do this.)

DAY 4

Take a five-minute walk, then make something using whatever materials are available where you've ended up. Leave it there for someone else to discover, but be sure to document it first!

What do you collect? Work with a collection of objects you have in your home (or borrow a friend's if you like).

Look in the kitchen and work with the first fruit or vegetable you spot. It could be in the form of juice, jam, or even canned.

DAY 7

One week down! See how fast it goes?
Today, make a stencil and use it in your work.

DAY 8

Transform an old book into something new
by cutting, folding, gluing, and so on.

Make something with your breakfast before you eat it.

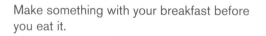

Use only water as your medium/inspiration today.

DAY 11

Work on the other hand. Pick a medium you're comfortable with, then work with your nondominant hand—if you usually favor your right hand then only use your left and vice-versa.

DAY 12

Camouflage. Create or alter something so that it disappears into its background.

Use tea leaves or tea bags (used or unused) or even just liquid tea (in a cup or not) to create something today.

Make something microscopic. How small can you work? Can you make something that requires a magnifying glass or microscope to see?

 **DAY 15**

Use a piece of paper currency as your medium or inspiration today.

 **DAY 16**

Make a unique print by cutting up a potato or sponge, and use it to stamp on a material of your choice.

Make something inspired by and/or that goes over an eye (yours or someone else's).

DAY 17

Work with the things you find in your car (or a friend's car if you don't have one).

DAY 18

DAY 19

Create something that floats on water.
(It doesn't have to be a boat.)

DAY 20

Buy or make some clay (see instructions on page 254) and then use it like you never have before.

Write a ten-word love story. Bonus: Illustrate it!

Create a bridge. Connect two things in a creative way. It could be small enough for an amoeba or big enough for an elephant to cross it.

DAY 23

Waste not. Dig in a recycling bin for all of today's materials.

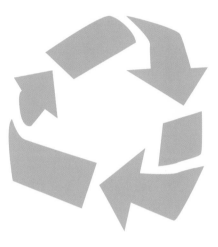

DAY 24

It's not easy being green. Work only with green-colored materials today. Try working on a green surface for a real challenge.

Work with nature. Go to your yard or a nearby park and collect materials to work with.

Make something portable (or that seems portable) that normally isn't.

DAY 27

Dreamland. Use a recent dream as inspiration for what you do today.

DAY 28

Back to school. Use traditional school materials like number 2 pencils or lined paper notebooks to make something nontraditional.

Make a disguise for yourself, a friend, a pet, or an object. See if you can fool anyone with it.

Play time. Work with toys: If you don't have any, borrow some from a friend with kids, and maybe even work with the kids!

DAY 31

Make a path for people to follow and invite people to try it out.

DAY 32

Make something ephemeral. Can you create something using a material that will dissipate quickly, like soap bubbles, smoke, butter on a griddle, or cream in coffee?

Use pens as your material/inspiration today.
Draw with them, use them as construction
material, or . . . ?

DAY 33

Work with wire. Thin-gauge wire can easily be
bent by hand, so no special tools are required.
You don't even have to buy wire if you have
some paper clips handy.

DAY 34

GET INSPIRED

ELIN WATERSTON created a relief print every day for a year (and since it was a leap year, she actually made 366!) . . .

Why did you decide to do a yearlong project?

I was inspired by two artists who were working on daily projects. One, of course, was the Skull-A-Day project. The other was Michael Lease's SAMETIME 7:15 photography project (see interview on page 170).

On average, how much time did you spend on each piece?

The average time was about an hour a day. That included drawing, carving, and printing, but I also spent a lot of time thinking of subjects and researching. There were some blocks that only took about ten minutes; the longest took about four hours.

What did you expect to get from your experience?

I really just did this project to see if I could carry it through and have the discipline to do it without missing a day. What I didn't expect was how much I enjoyed the comments and reactions from people reading my blog, where I posted my daily prints. I guess I didn't think about anyone

following it daily, just thought people would stumble upon it once in a while. But I had regulars who checked in every (or almost every) day. People also wrote to me with subject requests. That was wicked cool. It even inspired a few people to start carving or to start their own daily or weekly projects.

How did you stay inspired?

It wasn't always easy. Some days I felt like I was out of creativity, or that there were no subjects left that I hadn't already carved! The fact that I was committed to doing a block a day forced me to find inspiration wherever I could. Sometimes I worked on a theme, and that would keep me going for several days. I also asked for suggestions from blog readers from time to time. Sometimes I used other things I was doing at the time as inspiration—like when I was teaching summer art camp classes, I did blocks that related to those classes. But I have to admit there were a couple days when I got down to the wire and it was almost midnight then I just had to force myself to do *something* with or without inspiration.

What is the best thing that has come from doing this project?

I really enjoyed making connections with my blog readers. Some people left comments, so they were virtual connections, but there were others that I later met in the real world (at workshops or classes and once in a nightclub) who told me they'd followed my daily progress. That was quite a kick.

Any advice for people considering starting their own yearlong project?

I would suggest they try to develop a project that they feel passionate about, that they won't tire of, and that they can explore for that length of time. And just stay committed—there is a great sense of accomplishment once you hit that last day!

Elin Waterston is an award-winning textile and mixed-media artist. She has a BA and an MFA in design. Her art quilts are in many public and private collections and have been exhibited in numerous art galleries. She is the coauthor of Art Quilt Workbook and Art Quilts at Play and a frequent contributor to Quilting Arts and Cloth Paper Scissors magazines. Elin is an art instructor at Katonah Art Center in Katonah, New York, as well as an artists' model.

www.elinwaterston.com

Left to right: *Siren, Otto,* and *Galapagos Finch* prints. "I love bird imagery and use it frequently in all areas of my artwork. This one was made on February 12—Darwin Day, the anniversary of the birth of Charles Darwin."
Courtesy of the artist

DAY 35

Create instructions that others can use to make something and then have someone try it out.

DAY 36

Take something old and make it look new.

Make something with a stapler. You can staple things together or, heck, just work with the loose staples. Even the stapler itself can be transformed.

Work underwater. Fill up a large bowl, vase, or old fish tank with water and create something inside of it.

DAY 39

Write a haiku about something that happens to you today or is in the news today. Bonus: Illustrate it!

Haiku: A short, nonrhyming, three-line, traditional Japanese poem. When translated to other languages, they usually have seventeen syllables: five syllables on the first and third lines, and seven syllables on the second line.

Daily skull making
Reminded me to live life
By thinking of death

DAY 40

What can you do with yarn? You don't have to know how to knit or crochet; you can try yarn painting or just experiment.

Think big. Create a large version of something that would normally be much smaller.

Turn today's junk mail into something much more appealing.

DAY 43

Learn something new. Ask a friend to help you do something using a technique or skill they're good at.

DAY 44

Make something that lights up. Work with an existing lampshade or put a small electric light or candle inside of something you make.

Create an image with masking tape or any other kind of tape, for that matter. Try making it on a nontraditional surface. Extra credit: Leave it for others to find.

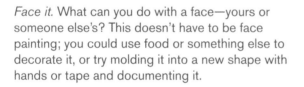

Face it. What can you do with a face—yours or someone else's? This doesn't have to be face painting; you could use food or something else to decorate it, or try molding it into a new shape with hands or tape and documenting it.

DAY 47

Work with flowers—artificial or real, live or dried, picked or bought.

DAY 48

How tall can you make something that stands up on its own?

Quantity over quality. Work with a lot of something. It could be dried grains from the kitchen, a jar of buttons you have in the closet, or all of your T-shirts.

Be a minimalist. Work only with white materials today. Try working white on white for a real challenge.

DAY 51

Make something that would not normally be considered cute and cuddly into something that is.

DAY 52

Work upside down. Create something in such a way that you have to rotate it 180 degrees to display/see it when it is finished.

Make something in which the sense of smell is the essential component.

Connect the dots. Make something only using dots. The dots could be stippling from a pen, the circles cut from paper using a hole punch, or even small, round price stickers.

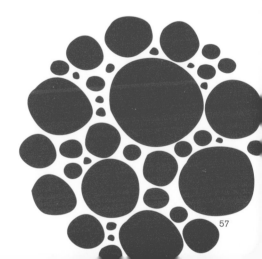

Write an advertising jingle for something in nature (a tree, a bird, a cloud). Bonus: Make a commercial to go with it!

Make something heavy seem light.

Use a disposable plastic bag to create something new today.

Life size. Make something as big as you possibly can! If it's something representational, see if you can make it life-sized (a giant cardboard elephant, a drawing of a person your height, a cloth car you could fit in).

DAY 59

Mix and match. Work with two materials that generally don't go together, like markers and bananas, or leaves and binder clips.

DAY 60

Make something that casts a shadow and document only the shadow.

Use only things you find around the bathroom to create something. Extra credit: Make it in the bathroom!

DAY 61

Make something with your dinner before you eat it.

DAY 62

DAY 63

Behind the mask. Create a unique mask with whatever materials you like. Bonus: Document yourself or a friend wearing it.

DAY 64

It's all about you. Incorporate yourself into whatever you make. It could be by wearing the work, by creating a self-portrait, or . . . ?

Work with only the classic tangram shapes.

Tangram: A classic Chinese puzzle composed of seven flat geometric shapes, which can be rearranged to make a variety of images, usually provided only as silhouettes. All of the shapes fit together as one large square and are often stored that way.

Go grocery shopping and pick up something new specifically to work with. Extra credit: Make the work at the grocery store itself. (Remember to buy anything you've radically transformed!)

GET INSPIRED

JONATHAN COULTON
started a yearlong
songwriting project
in 2005 . . .

**Why did you decide to do
Thing a Week?**

I had just left my day job and decided to try my hand at becoming a professional musician, but no one was paying me to do that, so it seemed to make sense to pretend that it was my job and manufacture this boss with deadlines. It seemed like a good way to create real pressure to do things was to declare the intention to do it on the Internet. If you have an audience, it's very hard to let that audience down.

**What was your creative process like
during each week?**

Every Friday was when I put out the song. Monday I'd wake up, and I'd pick up the guitar, and if there was an idea there I'd run with it, but usually there wasn't. So I would go and ride my bike, or go to the grocery store, or whatever it was, and then come back and pick it up. Once I actually had a thing to work on, I could usually do a recording in a couple of days' time . . . or, if pressed, four hours!

How did the year progress?

The first week, I did an idea that I had been kicking around in my head for six years, and the second week I had another idea like that, but by week five I was out of those ready-made ideas, and it got kind of tough. So then I had to rely on really half-baked ideas that I never really liked, or stuff that I manufactured out of nothing, or suggestions from people. And then, when I ran out of tricks in my bag in the last quarter of that year, I was running scared, and I think as a result I was really stretching out and writing some risky stuff for me. And that's my favorite material from the whole year! The thing I learned about myself is that I need to push myself, and when I do, good things can happen.

**What are the best things that came
from doing your project?**

This is my full-time job now, and it is literally a dream come true! It all springs from Thing a Week. Looking back on that year, it all makes perfect sense; I see exactly how I got here, and it was through those fifty-two steps! Left to my own devices, I produce things very slowly, and so compressing time in that way means that I now have a large catalog of songs, which is personally very satisfying, and artistically and professionally it gives me a lot of confidence.

**Any advice for people considering
starting their own yearlong project?**

Just start doing it. Stop thinking about

doing it. Stop everything you are preparing to do it. You don't need to buy another piece of software. You don't need to learn how to use this technique or this device. You already have the tools you need to start making the thing you want to make. Do not hesitate. It does not need to be good, public, or successful. It just needs to be done. The thing that got me through the difficult weeks was to say, "Your challenge was to write a bad song." And yes, you can write a bad song pretty quickly, but the trick is that once you start writing a bad song, you have started writing, and you won't actually finish the bad song, you'll write a good song. It's sort of a back door into the actual act of creating, and once the ball gets rolling, it's a lot easier.

An independent musician with the heart of a geek, **Jonathan Coulton** is a Yale graduate who left his day job as a computer programmer to stay home and write songs. Jonathan won the 2007 Game Audio Network Guild Song of the Year award for his composition Still Alive, which was featured in the critically acclaimed game Portal. All of the songs from the Thing a Week project are now available on CD, either individually or in a packaged box set, and his song Code Monkey is heard each week on the G4 television program of the same name. When not traveling the globe or using his powers for good, Jonathan resides in New York City with his wife and child.

www.jonathancoulton.com

These illustrations are by Len Peralta (www.lenperalta.com), who decided to accompany Jonathan Coulton on his Thing a Week project by creating his own image to go with each song. Top left: "Summer's Over;" bottom right: "Soft Rocked by Me."

DAY 67

Write a ten-word science fiction story.
Bonus: Illustrate it!

DAY 68

Create something with papier-mâché. You can buy
papier-mâché pulp and kits in art and craft stores,
but it's super easy to make, so why not give it a
try? (See instructions on page 250.)

Make a puzzle or make something using pieces from a puzzle.

Work only with numbers today. You could make an image using numbers, make something into number shapes, do something involving a calculator, or . . . ?

DAY 70

DAY 71

Time travel. Make something that seems like it came from another era in history.

DAY 72

Use all of the shoes in your household to make something, or work on a single pair of shoes that were destined for the thrift store.

Work with the gravel, sand, or rocks available near your home.

Be bold. Go to a store that you frequently shop at or a restaurant where you frequently eat and ask what they'll let you make there. You'll probably do better with a local business than a chain store, and if you're sharing your project, they'll probably appreciate the publicity.

DAY 75

Get some chalk and work on the sidewalk near your home.

DAY 76

Make something inspired by and/or that fits on or around an ear (yours or someone else's).

Work with shredded paper. Use an actual paper
shredder or simply cut paper into thin strips.
Maybe even give quilling a try. (See instructions on
page 251.)

Make up a name and write a back story for a
stranger you see today. Bonus: Create something
based on what you've made up and give it to them.

DAY 79

Walk through an alley or along a small road and pick up discarded materials to work with. Don't be afraid of a little dirt—just be careful not to cut yourself.

DAY 80

Try dyeing! Work with food or fabric dye. You can try traditional tie-dye methods or just paint it on. Experiment with unconventional materials.

Make something out of erasers. Kneaded erasers are great to mold, standard pink erasers can be easily carved, and straight pins can be used to attach them to each other.

DAY 81

Create a new kind of utensil. Functional or not, document it in use.

DAY 82

DAY 3

Make a visual pun. For example, a handbag made out of hands.

DAY 4

Keep it clean. Use a bar of soap to make something new. You can carve it with a knife, use it to draw, break it into pieces, or even make bubbles—just have fun.

Work with words. Make an image with just words or letters. You can cut them from magazines, draw them yourself, or print out words on a computer to work with.

Decorate a cake, pie, or cookie. Store-bought or homemade frosting can be used, but sprinkles, powdered sugar, and other toppings are fun to work with as well. Document it being eaten.

 **DAY 7**

What can you do with a candle? Try using the drips from a lit candle to make an image, or use an unlit one to draw on a porous surface, then make the image appear with watercolor or ink. Or, as always, feel free to experiment.

 **DAY 8**

Make something only using stuff from your workplace or office. If you don't work, use items that are usually found in an office.

Work only with bubble wrap or any other packing materials you have on hand.

Make a piñata and destroy it! (See instructions on page 253.) Bonus: Have a party specifically for the occasion.

DAY 1

Use dry coffee beans, dry or wet coffee grounds, or even liquid coffee (in a cup or not) to create something today.

DAY 2

Write a letter to yourself at another time in your life (past or future). Bonus: Send it to someone who is currently that age and discuss it with them.

Nuts and bolts. Make something with any nuts, bolts, screws, or nails you have lying around. Borrow or buy some if you have to.

DAY 93

Nothing rhymes with orange. Work only with orange materials today. Try working on an orange surface for a real challenge.

DAY 94

DAY 95

Ask a stranger for a suggestion of what to do today. Explaining what you're up to is part of the experience! Bonus: Get them involved in the actual thing you make.

DAY 96

Work backward. Work in front of a mirror, looking at what you're creating only in the mirror until you're finished.

Make an invitation to an everyday event you wouldn't normally invite people to.
Bonus: Actually send them out.

Work with time. Try making something that is only visible in a long-exposure photograph. Drawing with a laser pointer, flashlight, or a sparkler in the dark are a few options; you can even create an image by moving the camera itself. If you don't have a camera that can do the job, see if a friend can help.

ANJA BRUNT created a face a day for a year and is now well on her way to her next goal of making 1,001 faces . . .

Why did you decide to do the 365 Faces Project?

I wanted to try a very different project: one that was just for fun and didn't use the computer so much. I was already making small faces out of vintage woolen blankets as presents for friends. I noticed that small changes in a face can make a huge difference in its expression. It seemed like an inexhaustible topic to start working on.

On average, how much time did you spend on each piece?

Just a short time—not more than fifteen minutes. I love to work quickly. If you don't have time to think, it can lead to surprising things.

What did you expect to get from this experience?

To be honest, I did not have any expectations. I just wanted to do a playful project. I have been very surprised by all the positive feedback from people who liked my project. Moreover, it has given me some free publicity, like a spread in Australian magazine *Frankie* and a profile on Dutch national television.

How has this process affected your creativity/skills/style?

It has taught me to work more out of the box and trust my instincts and the materials I am using.

Do you think you will ever commit to doing another project like this?

Definitely! My next project will probably relate to animals and nature—the things in life I enjoy a lot!

What advice do you have for people considering starting their own daily/yearlong projects?

Choose a topic that is close to you. Otherwise, it will be difficult to sustain it on a day-to-day basis. Focus on pleasure; not every piece has to be beautiful or special. If there is no pleasure, there will be not so many surprises. And, last but not least, create an online platform, like a blog or a Pinterest board, where people can keep track of what you do.

Mini happy face from wool on autumn leaf.

Upper left: Collage of vintage
  paper stuff and found object faces.
Lower right: Cotton ear cleaner faces with
  pen and ink.

Photo by Paulus Veltman

Top to bottom: Vintage picture with clay face,
face made from found objects including an
old brush from my father, faces made from
found small caps from the street.

All images courtesy of Anja Brunt

Anja Brunt *is a graphic designer
living in Amsterdam, Holland, with her
boyfriend and two rabbits. She loves to
be outdoors, especially on the Wadden
Islands in the north of Holland. Her
favorite spot in Amsterdam is Artis Zoo.*

**365facesproject.blogspot.com
www.anjabrunt.nl**

DAY 99

Use the world of insects as your inspiration today.

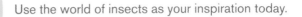

DAY 100

Make something new out of an old T-shirt. It doesn't have to be wearable when it's done, but if it is, document it while someone has it on!

Flip to a random page in a book at hand and make something inspired by the first sentence you read.

Write a palindrome. Bonus: Illustrate it!

Palindrome: A word or phrase that when read backward is the exactly the same as when it is read forward (though changes in punctuation and spacing are allowed).

DAY 103

Create something with the napkin (paper or cloth) that you use at a meal today. Extra credit: Leave it behind for someone else to discover.

DAY 104

Regress. Work as if you were a young child or baby. Use the materials they might have access to and/or with only the skills and abilities they have at that age.

Make something impossible. Can you trick the eyes into believing they're seeing something that they're not? For inspiration, look online or at the library for classic optical illusions.

Go to a thrift store and buy something to work with today. Why not give it back to them after you document it?

DAY 107

Have a ball. Make something out of a ball or make a new ball out of something else and then play with it.

DAY 108

Create something in the steam on a bathroom mirror or other steamed-up surface.

Play in the dirt. Go outside and create something in or with the first patch of dirt you can find.

Work with mistakes. Spill some ink, milk, or other liquid and then go from there.

DAY 111

Make a facial expression on your plate from the leftovers of a meal today. Bonus: Get other people to do it too! You can write expressions on slips of paper and have people randomly choose them to make it more challenging.

DAY 112

Work with a few free paint swatch samples found at most hardware stores and use them to create something new.

Paint the town red. Work only with red materials today. Try working on a red surface for a real challenge.

Make something out of toast or bread. You can even make your bread from scratch; recipes are easy to find online or at the library.

DAY 115

Find or buy a kit of some sort (like a plastic-model kit, a craft-making kit, or an electronics kit), get rid of the instructions, and make something that's not at all like intended result.

DAY 116

Create something using an old map or something that ends up looking like a map.

Go out of your way. Travel somewhere you wouldn't normally go today specifically to create something inspired by that location.

DAY 117

Make something out of wood. (Any kind will do: twigs, sticks, toothpicks, construction scraps, etc.)

DAY 118

 **DAY** Create an animal that has never existed before.

 **DAY** Make something in a box. (Any type of small box will do: shoebox, cigar box, shipping box, even a small suitcase can work.)

Do something with only tinfoil today. How many different ways can it be used?

Make a working musical instrument. It doesn't have to look, sound, or work like any existing musical instruments!

DAY 123

Work with or be inspired by an eggshell. If you want to keep the shell intact, make a pinhole in the top and a larger hole in the bottom. Then blow through the smaller hole and aim the bottom toward a bowl to collect the contents (be sure to wash the egg to keep it from getting stinky).

DAY 124

Make something seem like it is passing through a wall or other solid material that it normally wouldn't or couldn't.

Triangulate. Only work with triangle shapes today—or make a giant triangle with a bunch of stuff.

Make something that can fly and test it out.

DAY 127

Mail art! Take an existing postcard and alter it, then send it to a random address (or anonymously to a friend), after documenting it, of course.

DAY 128

Write a ten-word autobiography. Bonus: Illustrate it! Extra credit: Make a six-word version and share it at www.sixwordmemoirs.com.

Make a passport, travel poster, monetary unit, or other item for a fictional country or another planet.

Pick a piece of music you love (or hate) and use it as the inspiration for today's piece.

GET INSPIRED

JEN MACNEIL decided to do something new every day from her twenty-ninth to her thirtieth birthday . . .

Why did you decide to start In The New?

I was looking for an interesting way to ring in my thirties. My twenties were very interesting and productive, and I wanted to send them out with a bang. And I wanted to do something more original than skydiving. Since I couldn't settle on just one thing to do, I decided to do something every day.

On average, how much time did you spend doing these new things?

On average, about an hour. It got to where I would decide on something as much as a week in advance, prepare for it, then bang it out in twenty minutes.

Had you tried making a yearlong project before?

The only other yearlong thing I tried before was to read a "classic" novel every week. That lasted about a month, mostly because I didn't faithfully blog about it, so I didn't have that need to be accountable to anyone besides myself.

What did you expect to get from this experience?

I just wanted to finish my twenties in an awesome way, and I absolutely met that goal. Aside from experiencing 366 (leap year!) new and awesome things, the outpouring of support, the media attention, and the friends I made were overwhelming.

What have you learned about yourself in the process of doing this?

That I can accomplish anything, that crickets are actually a really good snack, and that I could never be a farmer, because castrating calves is kind of traumatic.

How did you stay inspired?

I kept notes, had a day planner full of Post-its, asked people for ideas, and kept in mind that if I didn't blog every day, I would be disappointing someone else.

Do you think you will ever commit to doing another yearlong project?

Definitely. This particular project proved that I can commit to something like this, but as I get to an age where I'm thinking about having kids, it maybe seemed a bit selfish. The next time I do another project like this, it will be to teach someone else.

Any advice for people considering starting their own yearlong project?

Start in your comfort zone, then gradually move out of it. Don't shoot for huge things right away. As you get into a groove of doing something on a regular basis, you'll know when to expand your realm and take more risks. And find a way to share it with other people, whether it's a blog everyone can see, or regular e-mails to a few people. Having that kind of accountability, and knowing other people are watching you, will keep you on task.

Anya Garrett

Jen MacNeil *is a performer and a freelance writer with a master's in journalism and a craving for the unusual. She has been a tube vocalist for Blue Man Group, a contestant on* Who Wants to be a Millionaire? *and a movie extra, and maintains the blog* In the New *which detailed her quest to do one new thing every day for an entire year.*

www.jen365.blogspot.com

Top left: Trimming a bonsai plant. Top right: "I visited a farm for a weekend and cut honey out of a live apiary. The bees were sort of scary, but fresh honey is really delicious." Bottom right: "I borrowed a saxophone to play on a subway platform. At first it sounded like a lot of farting. Later, it still sounded like a lot of farting, but I was pretty passionate about it, and it turned out to be tons of fun." *Kevin Danenberg | www.kevindanenberg.com*

DAY 131

Make a word out of objects in your environment or with letters found in natural formations outside.

DAY 132

Create something on a T-shirt and wear it for the rest of the day.

Make something surreal. (Look up the art of Magritte or Dali online or at the library for some inspiration.)

Reinterpret your favorite childhood story.

DAY 135

Make a rubbing by placing paper over rough objects and using charcoal or chalk to pick up the details. Gravestones are the classic source for this technique.

DAY 136

Create a life-size person using your clothes and/or whatever else you have at hand.

Look at the morning sky when you first get up today and make something inspired by what you see.

DAY 137

Make something inspired by a fictional character. Maybe it looks like them, or perhaps it's something they might own, or . . . ?

DAY 138

DAY 139

Make something that will decay over time and document it until it's gone (or too smelly to keep).

DAY 140

Create a rebus. Bonus: Try using real objects instead of drawings of them.

Rebus: A visual puzzle in which a combination of images, and sometimes letters, are combined with plus or minus symbols to lead the viewer to read specific words or phrases.

Make a paper pop-up. A simple pattern can be found on page 252.

Cut holes in the pages of a magazine or book so that what you reveal beneath creates something new.

DAY 143

Make something in which the sense of taste is the essential component.

DAY 144

Use your feet as your hands and/or your hands as your feet as part of whatever you do today.

Make something incongruous. Use an unexpected material to make something familiar (a feather made of wood, a stool made of sponges, and so on).

Create a visual definition for a word chosen randomly from a dictionary. Try choosing a word you don't already know!

DAY 147

Make something inspired by your favorite movie.

DAY 148

Purple people eater. Work only with purple materials today. Try working on a purple surface for a real challenge.

Work with all the utensils you own today.

Make something inspired by and/or that fits on or around a nose (yours or someone else's).

DAY 151

Work with crayons. You can mold them, melt them, grate them, color with them, or . . . ?

DAY 152

Create a chain reaction (a sequence of events in which one action prompts the next) or use the idea of one as your subject matter today.

Make something light seem heavy.

Create a simple board game and play it, ideally
with friends.

DAY 155

Use fingerprints/thumbprints to create an image or portrait.

DAY 156

Work only with toilet paper tubes and/or paper towel tubes today.

Make something that's strong enough to support your own weight and stand on it.

Work with homonyms today. Homonyms are words that sound the same but are spelled differently and have different meanings.

DAY 159

Use makeup—yours or borrowed, everyday or costume. You can work on skin, paper, or a nontraditional material.

DAY 160

Make a kit for an activity that normally wouldn't need one.

Work with an old calendar or make something into a calendar.

Create a trap. Think about what you'd want to catch and make something appropriate. It doesn't necessarily have to function or be designed to catch a real thing.

GET INSPIRED

vietnamese bánh mi sandwiches

I ATE THIS THREE LUNCHES in a row.
$3.50 each
4TH & HALL
1.28.10

KATE BINGAMAN-BURT has been drawing a picture of something she's purchased every day since Februrary 2006 . . .

Why did you decide to start Obsessive Consumption?

I started this project as a break from another project, where I was drawing all of my credit card statements by hand. The credit card project was not fun, but that also was *not* the point. Making work about consumption, and personal consumption especially, is a big theme throughout my work; drawing the mundane items that we all purchase every day just seemed like a natural next step. I also felt uncomfortable drawing objects, and drawing an object every day was the perfect way to get more comfortable.

How often did you make similar creative work before this?

I am a big fan of setting up rules and limitations for myself. Rules create freedom. The Daily Purchase Drawing Project is the third project like this for me. From 2002 to 2004, I photo-documented everything that I purchased. From 2004 to 2009, I drew all of my credit card statements. On February 5, 2006, I started my daily purchase drawing project.

What did you expect to get from this experience?

I just wanted to draw. I didn't have any expectations whatsoever.

What have you learned about yourself in the process of doing this?

If you do something every day, you get better at it.

How has this process affected your style?

My style has tightened up; still pretty naive, but more of a refined naive.

How do you stay inspired?

It's easy to stay inspired when you have a system of rules to follow. Also, it's easy to keep drawing when you are accountable to a system of rules.

In what ways has doing these projects transformed your life?

This is a hard question. I have been doing daily projects for such a long time that it *is* part of my life now.

Top left: "I really enjoy drawing food and packaging. 2010 was the year of the Banh Mi sandwich for me." Top right: "I render all of my drawings in simple black ink. I have been using this brand of pen for almost two years now." Bottom right: A navy blue vintage dress that Kate purchased forty-five minutes before one of her art openings. *Courtesy of the artist*

FABER-CASTELL
since 1761

FABER-CASTELL

10

$18.80

pitt artist pen

I buy them by
the BOX now.
3.15.10

What is the best thing that has come from doing this project?

Learning that I *love* drawing.

Will you keep doing projects this way?

I can't imagine working in a way where rules don't exist.

Any advice for people considering starting their own yearlong project?

Just make work. Don't stress yourself out over certain starting points or end points. Just keep making.

OPENING DRESS.
52.00   4.2.10
from flutter → across the street
from LAND.

Kate Bingaman-Burt *was born in Kenosha, Wisconsin, in 1977. She founded Obsessive Consumption in 2002 and has documented her personal consumption in many different mediums. Kate is active in the indie craft and craftivism movements. She lives in Portland, Oregon, where, along with being an assistant professor of graphic design at Portland State University, she also makes piles of work about consumerism (zines! pillows! dresses! drawings! paper chains! photos!). She happily draws for other good people too (IDEO, Madewell, ReadyMade magazine, the New York Times, Wieden + Kennedy). Kate also conducts zine workshops and spreads the craftivism word. Her first book, Obsessive Consumption: What Did You Buy Today? was recently published.*

www.katebingamanburt.com

DAY 163

Work with only the items you find in your refrigerator or freezer.

DAY 164

Use the wind. Make something that incorporates or requires wind to be complete.

Transform a piece of furniture into something other than what it's meant for.

Get medieval. Make a piece or suit of armor. It could be for you, an animal, or any object that needs protection.

DAY 167

Use only pencils as your material or inspiration today. You can draw with them, or they can be used as construction material, or . . . ?

DAY 168

Write a ten-word horror or ghost story.
Bonus: Illustrate it!

Create a personal shelter. What does it shelter you from? Can you fit inside it? It could even be something that's portable or is found at specific nonsheltered locations or events.

Make something unintended out of existing instructions (clothing patterns, model kit instructions, craft instructions, etc.) by not following the directions correctly, by using different materials, or by using the physical paper the instructions are on.

DAY 171

Work only in black and white (or with black and white items).

DAY 172

Make a book out of something other than paper.

Create a new traffic sign. Don't post it in a public space without permission, though!

Work only with kitchen tools today.

DAY 173

DAY 174

125

DAY 175

Miniaturize. Create a tiny version of something that would normally be much bigger.

DAY 176

Make somewhere indoors seem like it is outdoors.

Make a robot out of everyday objects.

Use the world of birds as your inspiration today.

DAY 179

Grow it. Use seeds to make something. You could plant them in a shape and document them growing, use the seeds themselves to make an image, or . . . ?

DAY 180

Be unseasonal. Create something that belongs to another season of the year and put it into the environment. Extra credit: Document what happens when others encounter it.

Use bones, skulls, and/or skeletons as your inspiration today.

Work with your hands . . . literally. You can decorate them using paint or henna, or even make a hand shadow. You might need a friend to lend you a hand. (Sorry, I couldn't resist.)

DAY 183

Make a hat and wear it for the rest of the day.

DAY 184

Use a skyline of your hometown or another city as inspiration today.

Yellow magic. Work only with yellow materials today. Try working on a yellow surface for a real challenge.

Make something quiet today.

DAY 187 Use a paper bag to create something new today.

DAY 188 Make something with your lunch before you eat it.

Write a joke or short, humorous poem about yourself or your hometown.

Work with newspaper to make the biggest thing you can.

GET INSPIRED

INES HÄUFLER decided to spend a year doing a wide range of different creative activities every day in her Be Creative project . . .

Why did you decide to do the Be Creative project?

I was working as a script consultant, mentoring screenwriters and production companies during the development process of feature films and TV series. One day I realized that while nurturing the creativity of other people is great (I love my job), I totally forgot about my own creativity. So I started a 365-day project in order to make creativity a regular habit.

What have you learned about yourself in the process of doing this?

Looking back, I think the major things I learned were about myself. For example, I found it was no big deal to push through all 365 days. If I have the right motivation, I can pull off something that seems like an enormous mountain in the beginning. I just have to start with small steps. I also learned to fight the ugly feeling of not being perfect. In the end, perfection is not important at all—it is much more about the process of creation. I tend to overthink ideas, which blocks me from executing them or from trying new things. And I realized that sometimes I have to focus on quantity instead of quality in the beginning, if I have problems kicking off the creative process. This is something I also found useful for work-related projects.

How do you stay inspired?

I love diving into art and books in museums and libraries and losing myself in the labyrinth of the internet. Also, we have a tradition of coffeehouse culture here in Vienna, where you can sit for hours and observe people. Inspiration is everywhere, when you open yourself up. I often feel like a sponge, and I cannot imagine that this constant flow of inspiration ever stops. It is around us all the time.

In what ways has doing a yearlong/daily project transformed your life?

The biggest transformation was that it set me on the path to become a cartoonist. It all started with a cartoon I made during the project, where I created a small comic with two real Christmas cookies talking to each other. The next year, before Christmas, some friends asked me if I would make some more cartoons with the cookies and told me they would definitely buy a book if there was one. So I put together a proposal and sent it to a friend who works at a small publisher in my hometown. She and her boss also liked it and a year later my first cartoon book, *Talking Cookies*, was published. In 2015, my second cartoon book, *Talking Pasta*, was published.

Top left: The little comic that started it all. The results are these two cartoon books so far. Top right: Poor pomegranate! But playing with food can be a lot of fun. Above: This series emerged quite early in the project, and I had a lot of fun coming back to it. *All images courtesy of Ines Häufler*

What advice do you have for people considering starting their own daily/yearlong projects?

Do not overthink it; just start being creative. Take small steps. Challenge yourself by trying new techniques and skills—most of the time the process is much more important than the result. And have fun on your adventure!

Ines Häufler *was born in Salzburg, Austria. After finishing her studies in German literature and communication science, Ines worked as an assistant director in various theaters in Germany and Austria before she moved to Vienna to start her career as a script consultant for TV movies and feature films. Storytelling is her passion, and she is now the author of two cartoon books.*

www.ineshaeufler.com
www.ineshaeufler.com/category/becreative365/

DAY 191

Be sweet! Use sugar as your medium or inspiration today. It could be loose, in cubes, in packets, or even used as glue when a bit of water is added. Bonus: Eat what you've made!

DAY 192

Make a family crest for your own family. If you already have one, make one for a friend's family or even a fictional one.

Build a puppet (sock puppet, paper-bag puppet, marionette, stick puppet, shadow puppet, etc.). Bonus: Create a performance with the puppet . . . maybe even get your friends to make other puppets and join in!

DAY 193

Make something that is supposed to be walked on, and walk on it! It could be a type of floor covering, something that attaches to your feet, or . . . ?

DAY 194

DAY 195 Create a monster that has never existed before.

DAY 196 Write a ten-word fantasy story. Bonus: Illustrate it!

Make something inspired by and/or that goes over a mouth (yours or someone else's).

Diagram a new dance step and teach it to others.

DAY 199

Make a flag for a new country or a new flag for your current country.

DAY 200

Save the hair from your next haircut and work with it (or get a friend to save you theirs if you're not squeamish). Or, if you have pets, work with the hair they shed.

Build a pair of eyeglasses. Wear them for a day. If you already wear eyeglasses, put the new pair over them or use your own as a base to work on.

Take something new and make it look old.

DAY 203

Make a map of (or to) a fictional place.
Bonus: Use it and see where you end up!

DAY 204

Ask a friend you haven't talked to in a while for a suggestion of what to do today. Explaining what you're up to is part of the experience. Bonus: Get your friend involved in the actual thing you make.

Make a meal that doesn't look like what it actually is and serve it to friends.

Look at the sky after the sun goes down today and make something inspired by what you see.

DAY 207

Use paper like it was fabric. You can weave it or sew on it—what else?

DAY 208

Create an inkblot print. Put a small amount of ink or paint on a piece of paper, fold it in half, and press the halves together, then open it to reveal the image. Bonus: Show it to your friends, and have them describe what images they see in it.

Create a package for something that's normally unwrapped.

Make something inside of a bottle of any size (soda, medicine, syrup, etc.).

DAY 210

145

DAY 211

Make up a new holiday for today and create a decoration, food item, or card to go along with it. Bonus: Get your friends to celebrate it with you.

DAY 212

Use the world of fish as your inspiration today.

Is there a doctor in the house? Use only the things you would find in a first-aid kit (bandages, gauze, burn creams, etc.).

Get the point. Use toothpicks as your main material or inspiration today.

DAY 215

Legal graffiti. Create an image on a wall using water sprayed from a squirt gun or spray bottle. Document it disappearing.

DAY 216

Work with light. Create an image using any light source in your home. One option is taking strings of holiday lights and creating an image with them.

Create a flip-book animation in the corner of a notebook or book.

Today, only work with or be inspired by measuring devices and units of measurement.

DAY 219

Create a mosaic using cut paper. Snippets of color from magazines are ideal for this.

DAY 220

Nothing but blue skies. Work only with blue materials today. Try working on a blue surface for a real challenge.

Use a tree (or trees) as your only material or inspiration today.

Make something appetizing seem unappetizing (but still edible).

GET INSPIRED

MELISSA OSBURN decided to paint her nails with a unique design every day for an entire year . . .

Why did you decide to do this?
It was a pretty simple decision, actually. I went a little overboard with the purchasing of nail polish (seventy bottles in about one-and-a-half months), and I really felt the need to justify that purchase in some way. I've done crazy nail designs since I was thirteen or fourteen, so it wasn't that far of a stretch, but never daily, and never this in-depth.

On average, how much time did you spend on each design?
The designs really vary in length of time spent. Some take five to ten minutes, and others take as long as two hours.

Had you tried making a yearlong project before?
No, this is my first yearlong experience, and I have to say, it's way tougher than I ever imagined, but the work is far outweighed by the awesome positive response.

What have you learned about yourself in the process of doing this?
A few things, actually. One being the fact that if you repeatedly do something day after day with your left hand, you will eventually work toward becoming ambidextrous. I've also learned the ways to push myself toward not being a procrastinator, and how to delve further into the creative puddle in my brain.

How do you stay inspired?
My inspiration comes from all around me, from my hobbies, television, movies, food, my job, holidays. I'll admit though, there *are* days where I have a really hard time getting inspired.

What is the best thing that has come from doing this project?
I've not yet completed the project, but I already feel a huge sense of accomplishment. I sometimes doubted that I'd get this far, but I have! I'm the sort of person that has about fifty projects started, but nothing ever gets completed. I have half-embroidered samplers, baby afghans that were started and abandoned, screen-printing equipment that gathers dust, bin upon bin of stained glass begging to be cut and soldered, and woodworking tools that haven't left their boxes in the two years since I moved to Las Vegas. I'm really proud and excited that this is a project that I'm going to start and *finish*, and an ambitious one at that!

Any advice for people considering starting their own yearlong project?
Make sure you're interested in what you're going to be working on for the next 365 days; otherwise, it will become a chore, and who likes those?

Top to bottom: *Bacon Is Great!*, *What Are You Hup . . . TO . . . 3 . . . 4?*, and *Rubber Ducky, You're the One . . .* "This last design was probably one of my more time-consuming ones—it took me nearly two hours." *Courtesy of the artist*

Melissa Osburn *is a nail polish hoarder, pizza aficionado, and devoted dog parent to her pups, Homer and Molly. Since returning to the United States from her year living abroad in India, she works full time doing social media for Zappos.com and spends her free time painting her nails, binge-watching bad TV, and cruising around in her lemon-yellow MINI named Marge.*

www.thedailynailblog.com

DAY 23

Create a fill-in-the-blanks story (remove nouns, adjectives, adverbs, and other parts of speech and replace them with blank lines), and have a friend fill it in. Bonus: Illustrate the end result.

DAY 24

Get dirty. Use dirt as your medium or inspiration today. It can be loose, in clumps, or even made into mud if you want to get extra dirty!

Make a unique birdhouse (or bat house, or doghouse, or cathouse, or squirrel house). It doesn't have to be functional. Extra credit: Document it in use.

52 pickup. Use a deck of cards to make something today, or make a unique playing card, or really challenge yourself and make an entirely original deck of cards.

DAY 227 Transform a room into a new environment—temporarily or permanently!

DAY 228 *Be balanced.* Work with the weights of things to create something that's perfectly balanced on a small point. Extra credit: Document it falling apart when it is pushed or otherwise made to be off-balance.

Work with or be inspired by a bicycle or parts from one.

Make a container, such as a bowl, bottle, cup, or box. What would it be used for? It doesn't have to be functional. Bonus: Document it in use, functional or not.

DAY 231

Create a new superhero. What are his/her/its powers? What does the costume look like? Bonus: Dress up as that character!

DAY 232

Make a cloud, or make something inspired by clouds.

Create a portmanteau and use it. Bonus: Illustrate it! Extra credit: Get others to use it as well!

Portmanteau: A new word created by sticking together parts of two preexisting words, whose meaning is basically a blend of the two original words. A well-known portmanteau is *spork,* which is a combination of *spoon* and *fork.*

Make alternative labels (name tags, can labels, descriptive stickers, museum tags) for things in your home and apply or use them. Bonus: Get permission to do this in a public space, such as a store, as well.

DAY 235

Use only the human body (your own and/or your friends') to make something today.

DAY 236

Carry something with you all day—preferably something you've made—and document it in a variety of locations.

Make a unique bookmark. Bonus: Leave it in a book at a library or bookstore for someone to find.

DAY **237**

Make a mural, big or small, with any medium you like. Make it on fabric or paper if you don't have a wall to use or can't get permission to make a permanent one somewhere.

DAY **238**

DAY 239

Desaturate. Create the illusion that the color has been removed from something so that it looks like a black-and-white photograph.

DAY 240

Make something with disposable chopsticks. Or make unique chopsticks out of something else and try them out!

Make up a new sport and convince others to play it with you.

Use only markers as your material or inspiration today. You can draw with them, or they can be used as construction material, or . . . ?

 **243**

Make a postage stamp or make something out of stamps. Bonus: Mail it! (Be sure to put real postage on there too, so as not to annoy the post office!)

  **244**

Get framed. Make or buy a frame and use it to showcase something that already exists so people can see it in a new way.

Defy gravity. Create the illusion that the world has been turned sideways or upside down, or that something is floating.

Use a sewing machine or a needle and thread. If you've sewn before, try a new technique. If you've never sewn before, don't be daunted—it's not hard to do a basic running stitch (see diagram).

DAY 247

Hide and seek. Make something that someone else has to find. Provide a map or clues to lead seekers to the location where it's hidden.

DAY 248

Open a random drawer where you live or work and create something with just the contents.

Make something out of or inspired by popcorn—popped, unpopped, or both.

DAY 249

Narrow your focus. Pick a small area indoors or outdoors and inspect it very carefully. Use the details you would normally overlook to inspire you.

DAY 250

Make a pair of shoes out of an unexpected material. They don't have to be functional. Extra credit: Wear them in public!

Be unnatural. Work only with natural materials to make something that would not normally be found in nature.

Create something that can transport you across a room. Bonus: See if you can construct it so that it can transport you *and* a friend!

DAY 253

Be animal friendly. Create something involving, or inspired by, a pet (yours or a friend's). It could be something for them to wear, a scene for them to appear in, or . . . ?

DAY 254

GET INSPIRED

MICHAEL K. LEASE and **BRAD WALKER** worked together on a daily project in which they each took a photograph, at 7:15 p.m. exactly, in their respective cities, and shared the results side-by-side online for an entire year . . .

What was the impetus for SAMETIME 7:15?

Michael: We wanted to work collaboratively, but we were interested in taking it a step beyond a one-off project. I was interested in how the factor of committing for an entire year would affect the work made and was looking for a degree of intensity from the project.

Brad: We decided it would be interesting if we took our pictures at the exact same time because our thinking was that the choreographed shooting would be a way to spend time together while seeing pictures that showed how clearly different our lives were (Brad being in Baltimore, Michael being in Richmond).

Had you tried making a yearlong project before?

Michael: In 1997, I drew daily self-portraits for (nearly) a year with ink on blank postcards, and sent them to a friend in New York City. I got really close to completing the project, but didn't make it.

Brad: I have done it every year since we finished that first year. The initial experience was perhaps the most interesting, since it was a fresh concept to me. Seeing the project age might be more invigorating than the initial snapping of daily photographs. This is why I continue to take daily photographs—the significance of the memories grows with time.

What did you expect to get from this experience?

Michael: I expected to learn what it was to work closely with another person on a creative project, while relishing the mundane, celebrating the workaday, and using the Internet as an art space. My expectations were met, and then some.

Brad: I expected to have a unique dialogue with my friend and colleague, to remind myself how aesthetically pleasing daily life can be, and to be part of a discipline requiring me to take more photographs which is healthy for me. These expectations were surpassed, not surprisingly.

In what ways did doing a yearlong project transform your life?

Michael: It made me realize that despite all of the ups and downs, headaches, and major pains in the ass that happen on a daily and weekly basis, a year is a very small unit of time.

Brad: Having the discipline of doing what I love is great in the fact that I feel more of a reason to take images. Since I'm on my fourth year (and have no plans of stopping), I actually am a bit upset that I couldn't have done this from an earlier point in life.

Any advice for people considering starting their own yearlong project?

Michael: I think it's a good way to spend your time. It slows you down a bit and helps you concentrate on what's at hand. In the world we live in, working on something (or thinking about something) for a year is anachronistic. I think that's a good enough reason to do it.

Brad: Don't hesitate!

Top pair: *May 22, 2007*. B: "Auto repair waiting station." M: "In the land of barbeque, there are many images of hogs. S&S Caterers is directly across from where I work." Bottom pair: *May 24, 2007*. B: "A good old-fashioned nap." M: "This is on the façade of a restaurant on Bellevue Avenue—not far from where we live. When I see this word, all I can think to do is add 'Anna' to the front of it." *Courtesy of the artists*

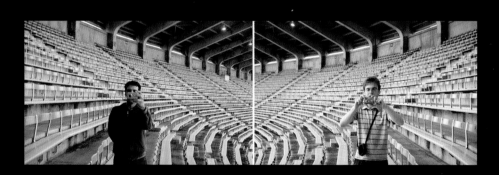

Michael Lease *is an artist and occasional adjunct professor in the photo/film department at Virginia Commonwealth University. On a regular basis, he is the exhibitions manager at the university's Museum of the Arts, the Anderson Gallery. Michael's solo and collaborative work has been shown at the Agni Gallery in New York City, at the American University Museum at the Katzen Arts Center, as a part of Site Projects DC, and the Flashpoint gallery in Washington, D.C.*

Brad Walker *is a graphic designer living in Baltimore, Maryland. He records music under the name Curtain Rod Character, has a zine called Majuscule, and is continuing his daily photography with five other photographers. All of this can be seen at www.bradwalker.org.*

DAY 255

Make a good luck charm. Bonus: Make it wearable and wear it all day!

DAY 256

Use packaging tape to make something three-dimensional.

Put pen to paper and draw for at least thirty minutes without stopping. If you get stuck, just doodle until an idea comes to you. For an even greater challenge, don't lift the pen from the page until the time is up. Extra credit: Increase the time to sixty minutes, ninety minutes, or . . . ?

DAY 257

Create an artificial window and install it in your home or somewhere in public. What can be seen on the other side?

DAY 258

DAY 259

Make something that would normally be considered cute and cuddly into something that isn't.

DAY 260

How now brown cow? Work only with brown materials today. Try working on a brown surface for a real challenge.

Start something, then have someone else complete it today.

You may have carved a pumpkin before, but what about a turnip, an apple, a bell pepper, or . . . ?

DAY 263

Make your own unique chess set. If you don't like chess, how about checkers?

DAY 264

Work only with Legos or other building blocks today. If you don't have any on hand, rather than buying them, why not borrow some from a friend with a child? Bonus: Try collaborating with a kid on this one.

Make a unique miniature golf hole in your home or outside and get someone to play it. You can even make the golf club and ball yourself if you don't have any on hand. Extra credit: Find seventeen other people to make holes as well and create an entire course!

Work with just corrugated cardboard or cardboard boxes today.

DAY 267

Recreate a famous work of art using the material and technique of your choice. If there are people shown, why not recruit your friends to participate?

DAY 268

Get sandy! Use sand as your medium or inspiration today. You or a friend can collect sand for free at the beach or from a sandbox, or you can just work at one of those locations. Craft stores also usually sell colored sand.

Make a pie chart, flow chart, Venn diagram, or other business graphic in an unexpected way. Perhaps it's made out of an odd material, or it diagrams something that's not at all business related.

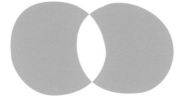

Venn diagram: A diagram of overlapping circles used to show the logical points of connection between two or more sets of ideas, items, or people.

Work with ice cubes today. Bonus: Document the piece while it melts.

DAY 271

Add a door where one wouldn't normally exist. Extra credit: Make it functional!

DAY 272

Make something inspired by and/or that goes over a hand (yours or someone else's).

Work with, or be inspired by, a tin can or soda can. You can decorate on it, shape it with tin snips, or punch holes in it with nails—just be careful with the sharp edges. Try adding a light for an added effect.

Go back to the future. Make something that seems like it has come from the future.

DAY 275

Use your pocket change to make something worth more than what you could buy with it.

DAY 276

Flip through an almanac or spin a globe and put your finger on a random location. Then research the place and make something based on it.

If you could do or be anything in the world, what would it be? Make something as if you were actually doing or being it.

Create something inspired by a piece of spam e-mail you (or someone you know) has recently received.

DAY 279

Be monumental. Make a monument to a mundane event, place, or person. Create a design for it or actually build it. Bonus: Place the monument in a public location.

DAY 280

Work with balloons, inflated or deflated. You could even use one as the base for papier-mâché, cover it in glue-coated string (let dry, then pop the balloon), or . . . ?

Imagine you are an animal and work as that animal would today (using four legs and a tail, with flippers, underwater, etc.).

DAY 281

Use a toothbrush and/or toothpaste as the central component of, or inspiration for, what you do today.

DAY 282

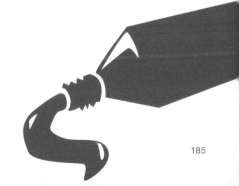

Make something that makes a sound on its own. Bonus: Record it and make something with the recording!

Make something that looks like it has been turned inside out.

Work with disposable plastic utensils you (or someone you know) have been given recently.

Do something in which silence is an essential component.

GET INSPIRED

RANDEL PLOWMAN has been making a collage a day since 2006 . . .

**Why did you decide to do
A Collage A Day?**
One of the main reasons that I decided
to start my project was to become more
routine in my art making. I also saw a few
other artists posting their daily art online
and thought that it would be a great way to
create an audience for my own work.

**On average, how much time did you
spend on each piece?**
I usually spend anywhere from fifteen
minutes to an hour on each collage.

**Had you tried making a daily
project before?**
I began a yearlong project called
Photo365 in 2009, where I shot
photographs on a daily basis. I ended up
taking more than 16,000 photographs.
I walked a few miles every day and shot
digital photographs in my neighborhood.
Now I'm thinking about doing a one-year
photo project where I shoot everything
within one block of where I live.

**What have you learned about yourself
in the process of doing this?**
Sometimes the creative process just
involves sitting down and beginning
something instead of thinking about it too

much. Getting started has always been
the hardest part for me, but when I start
working I'm OK. Often, I make my best
work when I don't feel like doing it.

**In what ways has doing a daily project
transformed your life?**
It has helped me to become a better artist
by being more disciplined. By posting my
work daily, it also gives me the opportunity
to have my work seen by people all over
the world.

**What is the best thing that has come
from doing this project?**
A few years ago, I was asked to curate a
book for Sterling Publishing titled *Masters:
Collage*. It will feature the work of more
than forty artists. I am also curating two
collage exhibits later this year.

**Any advice for people considering
starting their own yearlong project?**
The main thing is to stick with your project.
That is the hardest part, but also the
most rewarding.

Top to bottom: *Fields of Dreams*; collage on paper, 4 by 4 inches (10.6 by 10.6 cm), December 1, 2008. *You Said Something*; collage on paper, 4 by 4 inches (10.6 by 10.6 cm), October 22, 2009. *I Had a Dream We Were in Belgium*; collage on paper, 4 by 4 inches (10.6 by 10.6 cm), October 29, 2008. *Courtesy of the artist*

Randel Plowman *graduated from Northern Kentucky University with a BFA in printmaking. He has worked in collage since 1982, and his art has been exhibited in solo and juried exhibitions throughout the United States; in addition, his pieces have appeared in many public and private collections in North America and abroad, including the Cincinnati Art Museum. Randel's work has been cited in numerous publications. He has also curated several collage exhibitions and recently wrote and curated* Masters: Collage. *He teaches workshops in printmaking and collage. Randel is currently pursuing an MFA degree in printmaking from the University of Wisconsin-Madison.*

www.acollageaday.blogspot.com

DAY 287

Create an anagram of your name and illustrate it in some way.

Anagram: A word or phrase made by rearranging all of the letters in an existing word or phrase.

DAY 288

Make something inspired by your favorite television show.

Role reversal. Do someone else's job for part of the day and create something at their workplace or based on the experience.

Write a short love song about a pet (yours or someone else's). Bonus: Perform it for friends or in public!

DAY 291

Make somewhere outdoors seem like it is indoors.

DAY 292

Be square. Work only with squares today (or make a giant square with a bunch of objects).

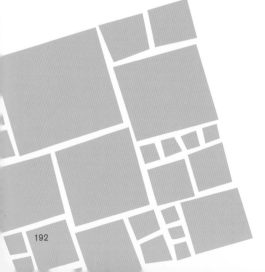

Get salty! Use salt as your medium or inspiration today. One idea is to make an image on a dark surface by pouring it out and arranging it with your hands or other tools.

Make something that is normally portable into something that isn't anymore (or at least seems that way).

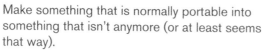

DAY **295**

Write a letter to a fictional character. Bonus: If it is a character from a book, leave the letter in a copy of the book in a library or bookstore.

DAY **296**

Go someplace where you would normally never do something creative and work there today.

Make something out of or on glass. (Any kind will do: lightbulb, window pane, television screen, etc.)

Put it in reverse. Try doing a normal activity in reverse order and see what can be made from the results.

DAY 299

Silversmith. Work only with silver materials today. Try working on a silver surface for a real challenge.

DAY 300

Make something in which the sense of touch is the essential component.

Pick a random date in history (day, month, year), research what happened that day, and make something inspired by the events.

Work only with, or inspired by, boxes or bags from packaged food products today. If you don't have any on hand, get some from a friend.

DAY **303**

Use the world of reptiles as your inspiration today.

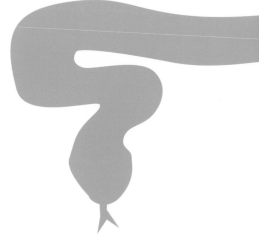

DAY **304**

Make chimes out of whatever materials you like.
They don't have to actually work.

Transform a piece of advertising so that is has a new message.

What can you do with a pad of sticky notes?

Create something based on the shapes
found in a plant in your immediate vicinity.

Make something that you can only see
properly from far away or at a great height.

Reinvent the wheel. Create something that can be rolled down a hill (with or without you riding in it) and try it out.

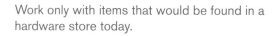

Work only with items that would be found in a hardware store today.

DAY 311

Create something that incorporates a mirror or reflections.

DAY 312

Paint it black. Work only with black materials today. Try working on a black surface for a real challenge.

Work just with matches, flames, or fire today (but be careful!).

Create a tattoo or something inspired by tattoos. Extra credit: Apply it temporarily to yourself, someone else, or even an inanimate object.

DAY 315

Get invisible. Create a clear version of something that's normally not transparent.

DAY 316

White or brown? Work with dry or cooked rice.

Make something inspired by and/or that goes over a foot (yours or someone else's).

Work with only rubber bands today.

GET INSPIRED

SHEENA MATHEIKEN decided to wear (and accessorize) one dress for an entire year to raise funds and awareness about the Akanksha Foundation, which helps educate slum children in India . . .

Why did you decide to do the Uniform Project?
The idea came out of professional apathy and a need to do something creative and consequential.

On average, how much time did you spend on each piece?
I improvise every morning, I don't really plan ahead. I've usually have about thirty minutes in the morning before I rush off to work. I find that the more serendipitous and spontaneous I keep the process, the better the outfits tend to be.

What did you expect to get from this experience?
I expected to raise a decent sum in funds for Akanksha. I expected to get some attention online, since it was typically the type of project that would perk up the blogger community. But I did not expect to get a call from the *New York Times* just two months into the project, or consequently from CNN or BBC or the tens of hundreds of magazines and blogs that have covered our project to date. And I certainly did not expect to raise the kind of money we have managed to raise. We now have close to $70,000 in funds for

Akanksha, and I'm grateful and thrilled about all the support we have received from around the globe.

How do you stay inspired?
Inspiration is such an intangible thing and sometimes comes from the most mundane sources. I also spend a lot of time online, and these days I find the majority of my inspiration on the web. I can get lost jumping around on Wikipedia for hours.

What is the best thing that has come from doing this project?
The people I have met, hands down. I have forged some incredible new friendships, people I probably would've never crossed paths with otherwise. I also fell in love with someone I met through this project. While doing an interview, in fact. It's been a delightful year in that sense.

Any advice for people considering starting their own yearlong projects?
The most important thing is that you are having fun. The minute it becomes a chore, it's over. If you're sensitive to this and know when and how to change things around, then you're not going to get trapped in the routine.

Math Problem

$10,000

=

27 kids
in school

How long will it take?

Born in Ireland, raised in India, and based in New York, **Sheena Matheiken** is the founder and chief architect of the Uniform Project (U.P.). Prior to the U.P., she worked as a creative director at an interactive ad agency in New York, with an MFA in design and technology from Parsons School of Design, New York, and a BFA in art from Stella Maris College, Chennai, India. Her experience in interactive design and media spans more than ten years and has been key to the positioning and viral success of the Uniform Project. Sheena is now looking to expand the U.P. into a global platform converging sustainability, fashion, and philanthropy.

www.theuniformproject.com
www.akanksha.org

perhaps a donation today?

Top to bottom: August 17—"We're inching toward 10,000. Let's get more kids into school." January 14—"This day Bungalow 8 in collaboration with *Vogue India* threw the Uniform Project a 'Sari Soiree,' where designers featured their reinterpretations of a vintage sari." January 13—"Spent the day in Pune [India] at various Akanksha schools in a pair of hand-painted Bata Keds and bangles that the kids handcrafted and donated to the Uniform Project." *Courtesy of the artist*

DAY 319

Write a ten-word murder mystery.
(Don't worry, you don't have to solve it.)
Bonus: Illustrate it!

DAY 320

Make a unique key and/or lock. Or make
something out of key(s) and/or lock(s).

Create instructions or a visual diagram for something that normally wouldn't need them.

Make alternate signage or images for men's and women's bathroom doors. Bonus: Convince someone to use them!

DAY 323

Work with only music media: old CDs, records, cassettes, eight-track cartridges, or reel-to-reel tapes, and/or their cases.

DAY 324

Make something that wouldn't normally melt seem like it has.

Create a wallpaper pattern using any technique. Extra credit: Install it on a wall or make a digital version for people to use on their computer desktops.

Use the world of amphibians as your inspiration today.

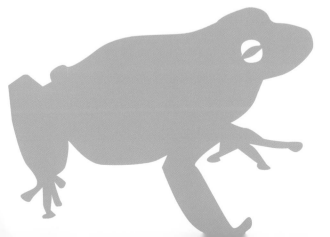

DAY 327

Create an alternate alphabet for a culture that never existed (from this world or another one). Bonus: Make something using this alphabet, like a sign or document, and leave it for others to discover.

DAY 328

Make something with a snack or dessert before you eat it.

Work with only tissue paper or toilet paper today.

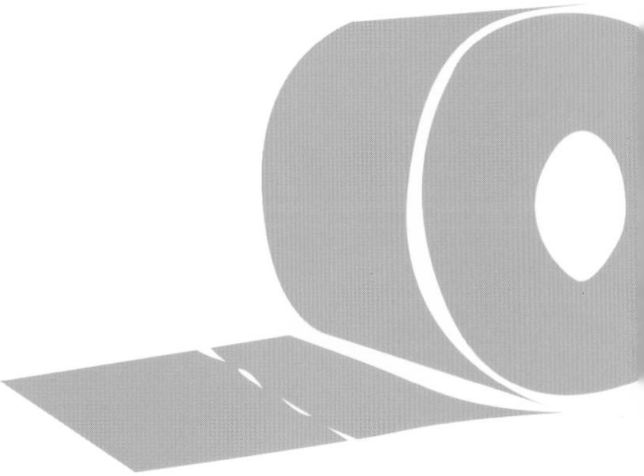

DAY 329

Time for finger painting! Don't judge yourself, and you'll be surprised at how fun it can be when you can't be precise. Use any substance—just be sure it's nontoxic.

DAY 330

DAY 331

Make a flower or other plant out of everyday objects.

DAY 332

Create a wheel chart.

Wheel Chart: Also known as a wheel calculator or *volvelle*, the wheel chart is a low-tech way to calculate or share information on detailed topics. You just need two circles of paper and a brass fastener to hold them together and allow them to spin. They can be single-sided or two-sided and can have several openings revealing all sorts of data on a subject. While wheel charts are meant to give useful information, yours could be filled with colors, images, random thoughts, or anything you like.

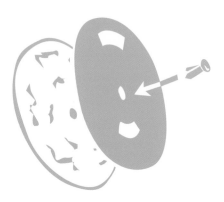

Make a unique trophy.
Bonus: Award it to someone!

Only work with bar codes today. Get them from items you own or make a new one out of an unexpected material.

DAY 335

Make a structure to protect a delicate object (like an egg). Drop it from a second-story window to see if it works!

DAY 336

Censor something that doesn't need to be. Show it to people and see how they react.

Work blindfolded. Pick a medium you're comfortable with and make something that you can't see until you're finished!

Be timely. Make something that shows the passage of time using any technique you like.

DAY 339

Create something that's only visible from one specific angle or location.

DAY 340

Work only with what's in your pockets today. Don't have any pockets? Work with what's in someone else's pockets!

Make a functioning mobile. It can be tiny or gigantic, in a public space or in a private room, just for you.

Mobile: A hanging sculpture that is intended to move freely. Generally, items are hung from rods or wires off a central axis and are balanced so that they swing around the center.

Create evidence of an event that didn't happen.

DAY 343

Make something boring seem exciting.

DAY 344

Use stars, planets, and other things found in outer space as your inspiration today.

Only work with the objects that are already on a table or desk near you today.

Make a repeating image by folding paper and cutting out the shape of an object or abstract pattern. Think of classic paper-doll chains and paper snowflakes as the inspiration for this one.

DAY 347

Add a face to something that normally doesn't have one.

DAY 348

Medium or large? Work with a disposable cup you've gotten recently.

Make something unappetizing seem appetizing
(but don't let someone eat it by accident!).

Have someone else start something and then
complete it yourself today.

GET INSPIRED

STEFAN G. BUCHER created an illustrated monster a day for 100 days . . .

Why did you decide to do Daily Monster?

For me, it wasn't a clear decision. I just started filming the Monsters for my blog with no clear plan as to how many I'd do. But the reaction was so strong and immediate—people sending in stories about each creature, as well as drawings of their own—that I knew what I had to do.

On average, how much time did you spend on each piece?

The early Monsters took about ten minutes to draw and another two hours to process and post. But the drawings soon got more involved and now take about thirty minutes or longer. And as soon as you add animation into the mix, the daily versions take up to twelve hours. Some of the special-edition Monsters can take weeks to animate.

What did you expect to get from this experience?

I expected to have a little fun and land a book contract for *Upstairs Neighbors*. Instead, I made friends with brilliant, creative people all over the world, got to make drawings for *The Electric Company* on PBS, paint a monster mural in Nebraska, make Monsters for all kinds of magazines, and publish a book about the first one hundred days. In other words, it was all a bit of a letdown.

What have you learned about yourself in the process of doing this?

A little bit of work done faithfully every day beats a short-term heroic effort by a mile, particularly if you set up a process that doesn't leave time for doubting yourself. I had no idea I could do this much work.

How has this process affected your creative skills?

The other day, I did some straight-up drawing from life, and I was happy to see that drawing Monsters every day actually revived my proper drawing skills too. Beyond that, the whole Daily Monster experience cured me of being such a Luddite crank. Before, I frowned at every new bit of technology as something unnecessary and only got on board months or even years after everybody else. Now I can't wait to see what's new.

How do you stay inspired?

I look, I listen, I pay attention. When it comes time to draw, I zen out and just let the ink guide my hands. The less my head is involved, the better the drawings are.

Any advice for people considering starting their own yearlong project?

Whatever you do, for the love of God, don't think of it as a yearlong project! Who in their right mind would start a project like that? Just start, and see where it takes you.

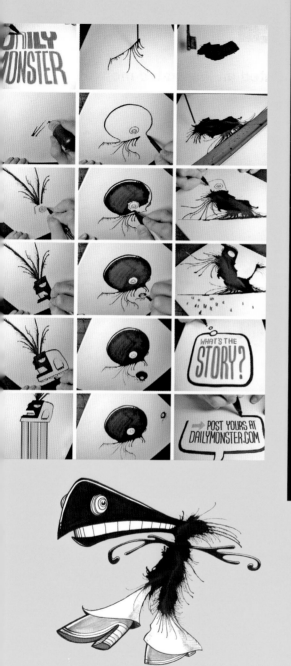

Stefan G. Bucher *is the man behind 344 Design and the online drawing and storytelling experiment Daily Monster. His Monsters have invaded computer screens all over the world, and their savage adolescence is chronicled in the book* 100 Days of Monsters. *He has created designs for Sting, David Hockney, Tarsem, and the New York Times, and he works with a whole roster of brilliant, driven clients. His time-lapse drawings appear on the rebooted TV classic* The Electric Company *on PBS. He is the author of* All Access: The Making of Thirty Extraordinary Graphic Designers, The Graphic Eye: Photographs by Graphic Designers from around the Globe, *and* You Deserve a Medal.

www.dailymonster.com

Top left: Still frames from the original filmed Daily Monsters. "I write the text and draw the Monsters upside down and in reverse, simply to show off." Bottom left: *Daily Monster 157*—"Many of the Monsters seem to have an affinity for Christian Louboutin shoes. Stylish creatures they are." Bottom right: Part of the Daily Monster Papers series on dailymonster.com. *Courtesy of the artist*

DAY 351

Add wings, fur, and/or a tail to something that wouldn't normally have them.

DAY 352

Design a uniform for a job that doesn't normally have one. Extra credit: Make it and wear it!

Goldfinger. Work only with gold materials today. Try working on a gold surface for a real challenge.

Work with only candy or chocolate today, wrapped or unwrapped.

DAY 355

Half and half. Take two things that don't go together and find a way to make half of one and half of the other fit together into one new thing.

DAY 356

Create a new book cover for your favorite book. It can actually cover the existing book, but it doesn't have to be a practical item.

Make something natural look digital (jagged edges, pixilation, made from ones and zeros, and so on).

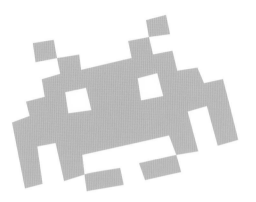

Freeze time. Create the illusion that time has stopped and something or someone is frozen mid-action.

DAY 359

Make a city out of objects you have on hand.

DAY 360

Use an internal organ as your inspiration today.

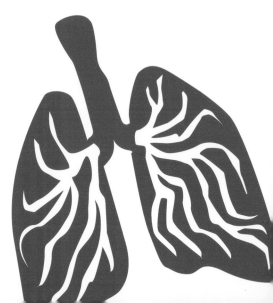

Work with bleach to make something by taking away color.

Make a rainbow from everyday objects. They can all be the same item (like book spines) or a collection of random things.

DAY 363

Extend an existing photograph or painting beyond its current edges.

DAY 364

Create a new birthday song or tradition. Bonus: Get people to sing or do it at the next birthday party you attend.

DAY 365

Make something loud today. And let everyone know it's the last day of your year!

BONUS MONTH

CONGRATULATIONS ON MAKING IT THIS FAR!

Many people who have gone through a yearlong project have found the experience so beneficial that they've continued creating daily well beyond day 365. And even those who stop at the end of a year (like me) may still need a creative boost every so often and a reminder of all the great things that come from this kind of daily practice. To that end, I've provided these bonus prompts to help you stay inspired. Feel free to start the day after you've finished a yearlong project, or just wait 'til you're feeling stuck and need a push!

What scares you? Make something inspired by your own fears. Bonus: Try something today you've always been afraid of doing!

DAY 1

DAY 2

Alchemy. Make something valuable out of something you consider worthless.

DAY 3

Who's your hero? Make something inspired by a real person you look up to. Or ask a friend to tell you about their own personal heroes.

Work only with string today, or use it as
your inspiration.

LOL! What makes you laugh? Make something
that's funny or inspired by something you find
very funny.

DAY 6

Curate it! Create a miniature museum or exhibition. Arrange objects or images, and add labels to them. This could be a private or public collection.

DAY 7

Make something specifically for a child. Bonus: Give it to a child in your life, and document what they do with it.

DAY 8

It's elementary! Use the periodic table of chemical elements as your inspiration today.

Whose birthday is today? Find a friend or a famous person whose birthday is today and make something inspired by them. Bonus: Give it to them or share it with them online.

Triskaidekaphobia. Research a phobia and create something inspired by one of them, or make up a new phobia of your own!

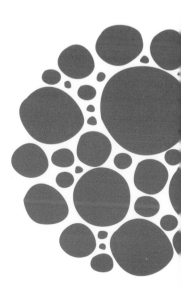

 **DAY 11**

Make a coupon for something that normally can't be bought. Bonus: Give it to someone and see if they'll use it.

 **DAY 12**

Create a vehicle that's never existed before. Bonus: make it functional!

Make something inspired by extreme weather
(hurricanes, floods, earthquakes, etc.).

Create a protest sign or banner for a cause no one
has heard of before. Bonus: Document yourself
using it in public.

Collaborate with someone else doing a daily
project today. Don't know anyone doing this?
Look for a collaborator by searching on social
media with the hashtag #CreativeSprint, or
encourage a friend to start a daily project (even
for just a month or a week) so you can do this.

GET INSPIRED

JULIE BERUBE set out to make a
year of pony-inspired art . . .

**Why did you decide to do the Field of
Ponies project?**
I was taking a break from fashion in
order to explore other possible avenues.
I was experimenting with illustration and
photography, amongst other things. During
that period, my mum gave me the first
edition of *365* and I thought it would be
the right kind of project to explore and
unblock something about myself.

**On average, how much time did you
spend on each piece?**
One hour on average, including the
photography and the retouching.

**How much/how often did you make
similar creative work before this?**
I had never done anything quite like this
project before.

**What did you expect to get from this
experience?**
Starting out, I thought it would be quite a
tedious and solitary project, but it became
something that friends as well as strangers
rallied around and it actually turned out to
be truly fun.

**What have you learned about yourself
in the process of doing this?**
I realized that having the guts to put
work out there—most of it being work
I'm not necessarily proud of in terms of
execution—to hundreds of followers every

day was in fact more important than the
work itself. What I understood is that, as
an artist or someone living a creative life,
having your own voice and not being afraid
of expressing yourself was half the work.
This is how you can provide entertainment
to people interested to follow the project.

**How has this process affected your
creativity/skills/style?**
I've learned to work fast and to trust my
instincts. I was making a point in using
materials that were available to me. I hardly
spent any money on the project. That way
of working has totally informed how I am
working now on my own clothing label,
which is quite against the norm in the
high-end fashion industry.

**In what ways has doing a yearlong/
daily project transformed your life?**
I came out of this project a completely
transformed person. I became self-
assured in my creative abilities and in
sharing my own voice. But most of all it
has forced me to reconnect with the child
in me, to just play and rediscover what
really makes me vibrate.

The project has given me discipline and
intuition, and those are the two assets that
are serving me the most in designing my
range, whether when developing new pieces
or styling a photo shoot or making business
decisions. It has paid off so far, with a great
stockist in Tokyo and so much support from

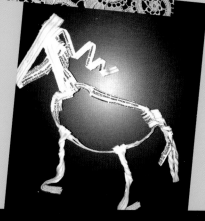

Clockwise from above: Petals pony made with flowers, Bread pony made of sliced bread, Twisty pony made of twist ties.
All images courtesy of Julie Berube

the press! Now I am ready to take things further and reach a wider audience with Field of Ponies, the clothing label.

What is the best thing that has come from doing this project?
The unexpected support and participation from my followers.

Do you think you will ever commit to doing another project like this? Why?
I probably will, because it gave me discipline and focus.

What advice do you have for people considering starting their own daily/ yearlong projects?
Share your project on social media. It will force you to stick with this amazing journey when days are tough. Be gentle with yourself; some days your work won't be that good and that's okay. Laugh about it, try to make it better the following day, or just leave it for what it is. Some days are more about a work in progress than a finished piece. The finished piece is the actual 365 items you have created together as a whole.

Julie Berube is a fashion designer based in London, England. Each sweatshirt of her label, Field of Ponies, is laboriously made by hand, and uses traditional craft techniques such as quilting, hand stitching, stuffing, and appliqué. She makes a conscious effort to reconnect with imperfections and celebrate their inherent beauty, including our own imperfections and the perfect asymmetry and randomness of nature, while maintaining a modern aesthetic.

DAY 16

Create something inspired by the world of exercise. It could be based on the movements and poses of a workout or inspired by workout equipment.

DAY 17

Make something inspired by the place you were born or a place you wish you were born.

Put clothing on something that's normally naked.
It could be an animal or inanimate object.

Make something that's normally drudgery into
something joyful!

DAY 20

Create something inspired by your
favorite (or least favorite) historical event.

DAY 21

Nocturnal. Make something that only
happens at night or in the dark.

Create something that loops or is inspired by the concept of things repeating over and over and over and over and . . .

What's that sound? Make something inspired by a sound or noise you love to hear. It could also be inspired by your least favorite noise.

Create and define a new slang word or phrase. Bonus: Use it throughout your day.

DAY 25

Make something inspired by laws, rules, or regulations. It could be based on a famous legal case, or legal terminology, or laws of science, or a rule you'd like to break, or . . .

DAY 26

This is a stick-up. Use glue as your medium or inspiration today. What can you make only using glue?

Create a space for something. Make an empty space that makes it clear what object, person, or animal should go there.

Unbirthday. Make and wrap a gift for someone and give it to them.

Work with musical notes and notation to create something today. The end result doesn't have to be musical or involve sound at all.

DAY 30

Make something with or inspired by dolls or action figures. Or make a doll or action figure of your own.

DAY 31

Make a certificate of merit for yourself or someone else. It could be for a mundane activity or something great that's gone unrecognized. You could even award it to yourself for completing this daily project!

HOW TO

A yearlong project is a wonderful excuse to add lots of new skills to your personal creative toolbox. The following are a few basic how-tos for some of the crafts mentioned in the 365 journal prompts. Feel free to experiment and create your own unique variations on them.

PAPIER-MÂCHÉ

One of the most versatile craft-making materials, papier-mâché has been around as long as there has been paper. This paper-molding technique can be used to make small items like beads or to skim the surface of giant sculptures. Practically anything you can dream up can be made out of papier-mâché.

Supplies
Newspaper
Masking tape
Bowl
Water
Flour
Paint and/or other decorating materials
Balloons or cardboard box, optional

Directions
1 Create a base for your papier-mâché sculpture. An easy base can be made by balling up newspaper and sticking the balls together with masking tape in the basic shape of your finished piece. For very large pieces, bent chicken wire can be used. You don't need to be precise with the base shape now; it can be refined as you go.
2 Pour a small amount of water in a large bowl and mix in flour until it makes a thick, creamlike paste. You can make more as you go along, so don't make a large amount, as it can dry quickly.
3 Tear newspaper into long strips and run them through the paste. Use two of your fingers to skim off the excess paste on either side of the strip so there's just enough to make the piece sticky. Place it onto your base and continue this process until the entire thing is covered.
4 Switch to smaller torn pieces of newspaper to create finer details and to smooth out the overall surface.
5 Let the piece dry entirely (which can take several hours) before painting or adding additional layers of finishing paper, such as colored tissue paper.

Tips
- Once dry, you can decorate it or glue other materials to it. You can even continue to change the shape by adding more papier-mâché.
- For a hollow base, use an inflated balloon or a cardboard box.

QUILLING

The traditional craft of quilling has had a resurgence in recent years. Quillers use rolled strips of paper to create everything from simple decorations to highly complex sculptures. It's an extremely easy craft to learn and probably one of the most inexpensive.

Supplies
Paper
Scissors or paper shredder
Improvised or purchased quilling tool, optional
Glue

Directions
1 Using a paper shredder or a pair of scissors, cut several long strips of paper that are the same width. Generally ⅛ to ¼ inch (.6 to .3 cm) is sufficient.
2 Roll each strip of paper so that you end up with a small, tight coil. Quilling tools are available to make this easier, but a hairpin or thin chopstick with a slit cut in the tapered end can be used just as easily.
3 Allow each coil to unroll slightly so that a spiral shape is visible when it is viewed from the side.
4 Close the coils with a small dot of glue—or leave them open if you want to attach two together to create other shapes. Coils that have been glued closed can then be pinched to create a variety of shapes (eye, teardrop, paisley, etc.).
5 Glue your coils together to create large shapes or patterns. Use different colors to distinguish different areas. Use unrolled coils to create lines or connect different pieces.

Tips
• There really are no steadfast rules with quilling—once you've made your coils, just experiment and see what happens. You can even incorporate other kinds of paper arts or nonpaper items.
• You can glue your finished creation to a board, have it be a freestanding item, or even make it on top of a dimensional base.

POP-UPS

Paper engineering is a complicated art form that requires a lot of skill to master. But there are lots of simple pop-up forms that can be created with just a few cuts and folds. And with a bit of decoration, they can seem far more complex than they actually are.

Supplies
Paper (any size will work)
Scissors
Decorating materials

Directions
BEAKED MOUTH
1 Fold piece of paper in half.
2 Cut a small perpendicular slit in the center of the fold. Don't cut more than halfway to the edge.
3 Starting at the corners of the cut part, fold the paper on either side of the slit against the main piece of paper so that it creates two triangular shapes. Fold them in the other direction to crease the triangles further.
4 Unfold the sheet of paper and then pull the triangle shapes toward you while simultaneously refolding the paper. This may take a bit of wiggling to get it to work; they can be done one at a time if need be. The end result will look like an open bird beak, which will close and open as the card is opened and closed.

Tips
- *Use sturdier paper for larger or more complex pieces.*
- *Try cutting into the shapes you've made or attaching other pieces of paper to them to create variations on the pattern.*
- *To hide the pop-ups inside a card, fold a piece of paper in quarters and use only the interior two panels for your pop-up; the exterior two will give you a solid exterior to decorate as well. Or you can glue your pop-up panel onto another piece of folded paper or cardboard.*

PIÑATA

The piñata is a traditional Mexican party decoration that has been a staple of children's birthdays for years. The festive container is filled with treats, hung from a tree, and broken open with a stick. Piñatas can be created as unfilled decorative items—but it *is* a lot of fun to break them!

Supplies
Cardboard box or balloon
Newspaper
Masking tape
Bowl
Water
Flour
Paint and/or other decorating materials
Scissors or hobby knife
String
Tissue paper, optional
Candy or other nonbreakable items for filling, optional

Directions
1 Start with an inflated balloon or cardboard box as a base. (You don't need to prefill your piñata, just don't forget to make a door or opening so you can fill it later.) Add balled newspaper, paper tubes, and the like with masking tape to make the shape you want.
2 Use the simple papier-mâché instructions from page 250 to cover the entire structure.
3 Let dry and then pop the balloon, if you used one.
4 Use whatever art materials you like, such as tissue paper, to decorate the exterior.
5 Add a couple of holes and run a string through them so the piñata can be hung up.
6 Fill with candy or treats, close up any doors with a bit of tape and cover with more of your decorating materials, and it's ready to use.

Tip
- *Rather than using candy, try filling the piñata with other nonbreakable items for a real surprise when it's opened.*

BAKER'S CLAY

Clay is a fantastically versatile medium that can be made with just a few kitchen ingredients. This simple recipe is completely nontoxic, so it's a great project to do with small kids. Baker's clay is definitely not a precision material, so have fun and experiment when you use it!

Supplies
4 c flour
1 c salt
1½ c water
Measuring cups
Mixing bowls
Cookie sheet
Oven
Paint or other decorating materials
Food coloring, optional

Directions:
1 Put 4 cups of flour in a large bowl.
2 Mix in 1 cup of salt.
3 Slowly add 1½ cups of water (add more if the dough is too dry and crumbly).
4 Knead with your hands until smooth.
5 Create things that are under 1½ inches (3.8 cm) thick or they won't dry properly.
6 Bake on a cookie sheet at 300°F (150°C) for 30–60 minutes to harden (just don't let it get brown).

Tips
- *If you want colored clay, you can add food coloring to the water before mixing it with the flour, or you can pull off chunks of finished clay and mix in a small amount of coloring (though be aware that it may stain your hands).*
- *You can paint or decorate the end result with most common art materials and even seal it with a varnish.*
- *This clay is not water resistant, so it may degrade over time if it is not fully sealed after it is baked, and very wet paints may cause it to soften.*
- *Keep the unused clay in a closed container, and it will stay soft for a few days.*

THANKS

A book about creative inspiration would not be possible without the influence and helping hands of others. Here are just a few of the people that kept me on the right track and are deserving of thanks: Mica Scalin, Paul Overton @ DudeCraft, Slash Coleman, Terry Border @ Bent Objects, Mark Hurst @ Gel, Andy Stefanovich @ Play, Mimi Regelson @ Exile, Erin Housholder and all the folks at The Video Fan, Nathan Wender, Shelia Gray, Tere Hernández-Bonét @ My Precious Studio, Madonna Dersch and Phil Cheney, Ross Harman and Oura Sananikone @ Sticky To GoGo, Lori Basarab, and Erin McKean, as well as all of the kind folks who agreed to share their work and experiences in this book!

A debt of gratitude goes out to Margret Aldrich and all the fine folks at Voyageur Press for taking on this book as I envisioned it.

Super-agent Kate McKean gets a heaping helping of thanks for once again guiding me through the murky waters of book making with grace and aplomb.

A very special thanks goes out to Citizen Agent, Justin "Tatman" Lovorn, and Abby Davis, who have taken on the reins of Skull-A-Day and allowed me to have the time to work on new projects like this. Plus extra kudos to them for each taking on their own weekly, yearlong skull-making projects as well!

My parents, to whom this book is dedicated, are the greatest art teachers in my life.

And my everlasting adoration goes out to Jessica, who has now seen me through the process of making two books and once again kept me from starving or ending up in the loony bin. Will you marry me?

Update: She said yes!

ABOUT YOU

_____

_____

_____

_____

_____

ABOUT THE AUTHOR

Noah Scalin is an artist, author, and activist based in Richmond, Virginia. He is the creator of the Webby Award–winning project Skull-A-Day, and his artwork is exhibited in galleries and museums internationally. Noah co-runs Another Limited Rebellion, an art and innovation consulting firm, and is a sought-after public speaker on creativity. He is the author of five books and the lead singer of League of Space Pirates, a rock band from the future.

NoahScalin.com

MakeSomething365.com

Photo credit: Bill Wadman